ESTRENO Collection of Contemporary Spanish Plays

General Editor: Phyllis Zatlin

FIRST STAR

and

THE RAILING

PALOMA PEDRERO

FIRST STAR
(*Una estrella*)

and

THE RAILING
(*El pasamanos*)

Translated by Rick Hite

ESTRENO Plays
New Brunswick, New Jersey
2001

ESTRENO Contemporary Spanish Plays 19
General Editor: Phyllis Zatlin
                  Department of Spanish & Portuguese
                  Faculty of Arts & Sciences
                  Rutgers, The State University of New Jersey
                  105 George Street
                  New Brunswick, New Jersey 08901-1414 USA

Library of Congress Cataloging-in-Publication Data
Pedrero, Paloma, 1957-
   First Star and The Railing.
   Translations of: Una estrella. El pasamanos.
   Contents: First Star. The Railing.
   1. Pedrero, Paloma, 1957-   Translations, English.
I. Hite, Rick. II. Title.
Library of Congress Catalog Card No.: 00-130964
ISBN: 1-888463-11-2

© 2001 Copyright by ESTRENO Plays

Original plays © Paloma Pedrero: Una estrella,1998, 1999; El pasamanos, 1995.
Translations © Rick Hite 1999, 2001
First edition

All rights reserved.
No part of this publication may be reproduced or transmitted in any form or by any means, electronic or mechanical, including photocopy, recording, or any information storage or retrieval system now known or to be invented, without permission in writing from the publishers, except by a reviewer who wishes to quote brief passages in connection with a review written for inclusion in a magazine, newspaper, or broadcast.

               Published with support from
            Program for Cultural Cooperation
           Between Spain's Ministry of Culture
              and United States' Universities

Cover: Jeffrey Eads

TABLE OF CONTENTS

A Note on the Plays, by Robert Graham Small ix

About the Playwright xi

FIRST STAR. 1

THE RAILING. 29

Critical Reaction to the Plays. 57

About the Translator 59

Rebecca Williams, Rick Hite, and Bob Nelson in *First Star*. Norfolk, 1998. Directed by Rebecca Williams.

A NOTE ON THE PLAYS

Paloma Pedrero is a remarkable woman of the theatre. She is a skilled actress, director, playwright, and a committed teacher of theatre. In this age of specialization, I have come to value those who are so multi-faceted.

Twenty five years of collaboration have taught me to appreciate the special qualities the actor/playwright brings to her work. There exists a true love for richly drawn characters--wonderfully complex people with tricks up their sleeves, eloquence on their tongues, and an uncanny knack for mischief and constant surprise. Such are the people who inhabit the two plays herein.

In *First Star*, we meet Estelle, a writer doing research for a novel. She is the only woman in a cheap bar. Men play poker in the back An elderly gentleman approaches her. He seems to know her. Does she know him? Is he just an estranged elder friend? A failed father? Maybe a little of both? This play opens up like the petals of a ruby rose. Once the bloom opens to full, it shrinks and closes again, leaving us clutching the thorns.

The Railing is a comedic look at the predicament of a handicapped man and his dutiful wife. They live in a second floor apartment, which he has been unable to leave for nine years. The landlady refuses to install hand rails! His cries for justice draw the attention of TV News. His plight captures the imagination of a city, as he becomes a symbol of the oppressed. But he gets more than he bargains for. By winning, he has lost the fight in his life. He gets exactly what he said he wants and doesn't need.

These plays do not come to English by some miracle of luck in translation. Rick Hite skillfully balances on the tightrope of accurate literal translation and free-handed adaptation. It is difficult to restrain the impulse to reinvent the play in a new idiom, and thus in a new voice.

That is not the case here. The plays are rendered as close to the writer's intent, with subtle shifts of image and syntax to make it viable for production. I have known Rick for twenty-five years. He, like Paloma, is a multi-faceted artist and an actor/playwright. Maybe that is why he is so sensitive to the sounds, rhythms, and energy of the text.

So, settle in, but don't get too comfortable. The people you are about to encounter are on edge. Their lives and their luck are about to change. So are ours. Change is inevitable, isn't it?

                                              Robert Graham Small
                                              Artistic Director
                                              ShenanArts & Shenandoah
                                              International Playwrights

PALOMA PEDRERO

ABOUT THE PLAYWRIGHT

Paloma Pedrero, one of contemporary Spain's most important and innovative women playwrights, was born in Madrid in 1957. An actress, director, and theatre teacher, as well as a prize-winning author, she has been associated with an independent theatre movement that wishes to explore, in realistic language, topics of concern to a younger generation of spectators. In her most recent works, she has extended her range of subjects to include older audiences as well. Her full-length and one-act plays are being staged with increasing frequency in Spain, Latin America, the United States, Great Britain, France, and other European countries. Some of her works from the 1980s, such as *The Color of August* (*El color de agosto*) and *The Voucher* (*Resguardo personal*), are already considered contemporary classics and appear in American textbooks of Spanish literature.

Typical of Pedrero's early dramas, like the ones that appear in number 6 of this ESTRENO translation series, are two-character plays that reveal a moment of crisis in a relationship and a search for identity. This group includes *The Color of August* and the one-act plays comprising *Nights of Passing Love* (*Noches de amor efímero*), as well as her first staged play, *Lauren's Call* (*La llamada de Lauren*). Her more recent theatre is varied in structure and theme.

La isla amarilla (*The Yellow Island*) is a fanciful, Brechtian satire of Western "civilization" from the perspective of "primitive" Samoans. It has been staged to acclaim in various theatres in the Madrid area by a unique acting group from a women's prison. *Locas de amar* (*Love Crazy*), a satire of what happens when a middle-aged wife is dumped by a husband in pursuit of younger women, was directed by the author at Madrid's municipal Centro Cultural de la Villa in 1996. In *Cachorros del negro mirar* (*Young Toughs*), 1999, Pedrero examines skinhead violence as well as the construction of gender.

First Star (*Una estrella*) has a cast of four, but like the early dramas, concentrates on the passing relationship between two characters. This psychodrama of a woman seeking to understand her dead father, an alcoholic gambler who neglected his family, was performed in France, Spain, and the United States in 1998. *The Railing* (*El pasamanos*) continues in the vein of social satire while giving a tender view of the loving relationship of a poor, elderly couple. It received its world premiere in Costa Rica in 1999.

Pedrero's theatre in general is characterized by its overt metatheatricalism, its frequent use of humor, and her constant questioning of traditional social norms, particularly gender roles. Increasingly she has focused on marginal members of society and serious social issues. Her skill at synthesizing dramatic elements allows her to create plays that may be staged with relatively small casts and limited sets.

Phyllis Zatlin

> CAUTION: Professionals and amateurs are hereby warned that *First Star* and *The Railing,* being fully protected under the Copyright Laws of the United States of America, the British Empire, including the Dominion of Canada, and all other countries covered by the Pan-American Copyright Convention and the Universal Copyright Conventions, and of all countries with which the United States has reciprocal copyright relations, are subject to royalty. All rights, including professional, amateur, motion picture, recitation, public reading, radio and television broadcasting, and the rights of translation into foreign languages, are strictly reserved. Particular emphasis is laid on the question of readings, permission for which must be secured in writing.

Inquiries regarding permissions should be addressed to the author through SGAE:

D. Alfredo Carrión Saiz
Director Departamento de Dramáticos
Sociedad General de Autores y Editores
Fernando VI, 4
28004 Madrid
Spain
Phone: 34-91-349 96 86   Fax: 34-91-349 97 12
E-mail: acarrion@sgae.es

or through the translator:

Rick Hite
742 Baldwin Avenue
Norfolk, VA 23517
Phone: 757-622-7631   Fax: 757-461-5025
E-mail: hrickhite@rcn.com

Una estrella was first performed at Saint Paul-les-Dax, France, on 24 February 1998. It was co-directed by Panchika Velez and Paloma Pedrero and featured Pancho García and Isabel Ordaz in the roles of Juan and Estrella. The touring production received its Spanish premiere on 28 February 1998 at the Teatro Bulevar in Torrelodones.

Una estrella was first performed in Madrid on 23 February 1999 at the Círculo de Bellas Artes with one change in the original cast. The role of Isabel was played by Mapi Galán.

First Star received its American university premiere on 26 March 1998 at Virginia Wesleyan's Hofheimer Theatre in Norfolk. It was directed by Rebecca Williams, and featured Williams and Rick Hite in the lead roles.

El pasamanos received its world premiere at the Teatro de la Aduana, with the National Theatre Company of Costa Rica, under the direction of Marielos Fonseca, on 22 October 1999. The roles of the elderly husband and wife were created by Mariano González and Anabelle de Garrido.

First Star and *The Railing* were given initial public readings by Theatre Wagon of Virginia in 1998/99.

First Star and *The Railing* were performed as staged readings at the 2000 ShenanArts International Playwrights Retreat in Staunton, Virginia.

FIRST STAR

CHARACTERS

ESTELLE TORRES, early 30s
JUAN DOMINGUEZ, mid to late 60s
RAMON, mid 40s
BARTENDER, mid 30s

(Translator's note: While "Estelle" is the translator's choice for "Estrella" [Star], of the original Spanish, either "Stella" or "Estrella" might be substituted should the director so choose.)

Interior of a bar. Stools along the bar. A couple of tables with chairs. A slot machine and an old juke box. The sounds of poker players float in from the next room. At times the voices rise with a contained violence, and we can make out a word or an occasional phrase.
  We see ESTELLE seated alone at the bar. She is a woman of thirty-something, slender, and with beautiful, long, red hair. Her dress and movement are elegant but unconventional. While she drinks her coffee, she observes the place with curiosity and makes occasional jottings in her notebook. She has a reflective and somewhat disturbed look about her. The only BARTENDER, who is behind the bar, watches her carefully and with a certain distrust.

BARTENDER: Sorry lady. We're closing.
ESTELLE: Closing? (*Pointing toward the back room.*) They have to leave first, don't they?
BARTENDER: Those gentlemen are members. After midnight we only let members in.
ESTELLE (*With irony*): Right.
BARTENDER: That'll be two hundred pesetas for the coffee.
ESTELLE (*Looking at her watch*): It's only a quarter to twelve. (*She jots down something in her notebook. The BARTENDER gives her a suspicious look.*) You've worked here a long time?
BARTENDER (*Wiping the bar*): A few years.
ESTELLE: More than five?
BARTENDER: Why d'you ask me that? What d'you want to know for?
ESTELLE: Don't worry. You don't have to answer.
BARTENDER: What are you writing down in that book?
ESTELLE: Nothing that would interest you. Some stuff of mine.
BARTENDER: You're not the police or something?
ESTELLE: No. I'm not the police. Relax.
BARTENDER: Some reporter type?
ESTELLE: That either.
BARTENDER: That's two hundred pesetas. I got to close up.
ESTELLE (*Taking out the money*): Just let me stay.
BARTENDER: What for?
ESTELLE: I'd like to see those men leave. From in there.
BARTENDER: I'm sorry, but–
ESTELLE (*Cutting him off*): Just a couple of them.
BARTENDER: That's not possible. You can't stay.
ESTELLE (*After a pause*): Look, I'm not going to complicate anyone's life. I'm a writer, see. I'm working on my next book, and it takes place in a. . . place, like. . . this. I need to get to know it, to know what a place like this is like. Where my characters spend their lives. You understand?
BARTENDER: A writer?
ESTELLE (*Taking a book out of her bag*): Look. That's me. Estelle Torres. (*The BARTENDER looks at the book jacket photo and then at ESTELLE distrustfully.*) You want me to show you my driver's license?
BARTENDER: And what are you gonna get out of being here?
ESTELLE: I told you. I need to get to know. . . the space. What those men in there are like. It won't take long. Just to see a couple of them leave. To observe them.

BARTENDER: I don't know. The boss isn't here tonight, and I got to work in there, too. (*Pause. Thinks about it.*) No. No, I can't.
ESTELLE: I'm not going to cause any trouble.
BARTENDER (*Looking at her closely*): Are you famous? You been on television?
ESTELLE (*Smiles ironically. After a moment*): Yes.
BARTENDER: Then you better go. This ain't a place for nice people.

(*The front door opens, and JUAN DOMINGUEZ comes in. He is a man about sixty-five. Short, thin, with bright, blue eyes. He has the look of someone who lives alone and isn't very neat. He greets the BARTENDER, who replies with an unpleasant growl.*)

JUAN: Where's the bossman?
BARTENDER: He's not here. Tonight I'm the bossman.
JUAN: Gimme a drink. (*The BARTENDER hesitates. JUAN shows him a bill. The BARTENDER grudgingly serves him a drink.*)

(*JUAN is drunk but still manages to keep his clumsiness almost under control. He has the look of the chronic alcoholic who carries an air of dignity about him. He goes over to the cigarette machine and gets a pack. ESTELLE watches him and writes something in her notebook.*)

BARTENDER (*To ESTELLE*): Hurry it up. I don't want any problems. (*Exits.*)

(*JUAN goes back to his drink, keeping his eyes on ESTELLE, who has her back to him. He opens the pack of cigarettes and taps some out and offers them to ESTELLE, who turns to look at him.*)

JUAN: You want a cigarette, Miss?
ESTELLE: No, thanks.
JUAN (*Pulling another crumpled pack from his pocket*): You smoke black tobacco?
ESTELLE: No, I smoke the others, but I don't feel like smoking right now. Thanks.

(*JUAN remains silent for a moment, watching her. ESTELLE turns away from him. He moves around and approaches her from the other side.*)

JUAN: Sorry to bother you. . . (*He staggers slightly, almost spilling his drink on her.*)
ESTELLE: Careful.
JUAN: Excuse me, Miss. I'm a little–
ESTELLE (*Not letting him finish*): You're excused. (*She turns away from him again.*)

(*The BARTENDER comes back in and starts to sweep up briefly, then exits again at some point. JUAN comes around to face ESTELLE again.*)

JUAN: Correct me if I'm wrong, but aren't you Estelle? Little Estelle.

ESTELLE (*Looks at him, surprised*): Yes. My name is. . . (*She notices her book still lying on the bar. She nods coldly.*) My name is Estelle. (*She puts the book back into her bag.*)
JUAN: I'm Juan. Juan Dominguez.
ESTELLE (*Hasn't the foggiest*): Nice to meet you.
JUAN: You haven't heard of me?
ESTELLE: No. I'm sorry.
JUAN: Maybe you just don't remember. But I remember you perfectly. You haven't changed a bit. Same red hair. You used to be a very pretty little girl. Now you're a very pretty woman. With that look. . . that lost look. . . with that mix of insolence.
ESTELLE (*Ill at ease*): So, who are you? If you don't mind telling me.
JUAN: I was an old friend of your father, Torres.

(*ESTELLE is momentarily stunned, then reacts violently.*)

ESTELLE: I'm sorry. I don't remember him or you!
JUAN: Don't tell me you're still angry at Torres?
ESTELLE: What are you talking about?
JUAN: Yeah. He told me all about that day. He was so hurt he had to tell me. He was knocked for a loop. "Dominguez," he said, "my little girl insulted me. She called me– "
ESTELLE (*Cutting him off sharply*): I told you I don't remember him. It's that simple: he's out of my life.
JUAN: What are you doing here? (*She doesn't answer.*) Here, have a cigarette.
ESTELLE: I don't want a cigarette. I don't want to talk to you. Do you understand?
JUAN: You're a spoiled brat. A little girl who won't grow up. An unhappy little girl.
ESTELLE: Just leave me alone.
JUAN: Why?
ESTELLE: You stink of alcohol.
JUAN: OK. I won't breathe your way. (*Touching her on the shoulder.*)
ESTELLE: Don't you touch me.
JUAN: My hands are clean.
ESTELLE: I don't like drunks touching me. OK? They piss. They wipe slobber from their mouths. They don't wash their hands.
JUAN: I'm sorry. I don't follow you.
ESTELLE: I'm asking you to leave me in peace.
JUAN: Even if I left now, you wouldn't be in peace.
ESTELLE (*Uneasy*): Either you stop bothering me, or I'll have them throw you out of here.
JUAN: You treat me like a dog.
ESTELLE (*Almost screaming*): Leave me alone!
BARTENDER (*Coming back in*): What's going on? Is he bothering you?
ESTELLE: Yes!
BARTENDER (*To JUAN*): I don't like you coming in here drunk.
JUAN: I'm not drunk. I was only trying to–
BARTENDER (*Cutting him off*): Come on, Dominguez. Finish the drink and get out of here!

JUAN: You watch your manners, boy. I didn't show you any disrespect.
BARTENDER: Finish your drink and get out.
JUAN: It's early. I'm in no hurry.
BARTENDER (*Getting aggressive, he grabs JUAN's drink*): Then get out and don't finish it. Come on. Out!
JUAN: Wait a minute. Do I pay or don't I?
BARTENDER: Meaning?
JUAN (*Handing him money*): Meaning if I pay, I stay and have a nice, quiet drink. And show a little respect. I could be your father.

(*ESTELLE watches him.*)

BARTENDER: What you ought to do is go find a bench and sleep it off.
JUAN: And what you ought to do is muzzle your yap.
BARTENDER: Get out of here now before you piss me off.
JUAN (*Beaten, but finding his voice*): You are humiliating me in front of. . . little Estelle, and I won't let you do that!
BARTENDER (*Violent*): I said get out!
JUAN: I've been coming here thirty years and. . . You wouldn't dare talk to me like that if the boss was here.

(*The BARTENDER grabs him roughly, wrestling him towards the door. JUAN lets out a groan of pain.*)

JUAN: Let go o' me! Let go o' me!

(*ESTELLE watches horrified. She jumps off the stool and crosses to them.*)

ESTELLE: Let him go! You're hurting him!
BARTENDER (*Without letting him go*): Nothing hurts guys like this.
ESTELLE: I said let go of him. Now!

(*The BARTENDER lets go of JUAN and looks hard at ESTELLE.*)

ESTELLE: What gives you the right to treat people like this?
BARTENDER: But didn't you just tell me he was bothering you?
ESTELLE: Well now you're the one bothering me. Like some vulture after road-kill.
JUAN: If that "road kill" was meant for me–
BARTENDER: You shut up!
JUAN: I don't shut up for anybody, and I don't think–
BARTENDER (*Wise guy*): You don't think what?
JUAN: I don't think, I just don't think. . . (*He can't remember what he was about to say. He pats the pocket of his jacket and then takes out a pack of cigarettes.*) Cigarette?
BARTENDER (*Disdainful*): Just finish your drink and disappear. (*To her.*) And you, too. I'm closing up.
ESTELLE: I'll go when I feel like it. And do us the favor of getting back to the bar. You've got customers.
BARTENDER: I did it to help you, lady.

ESTELLE: You're too dangerous to help anybody. Come on, back to work, if you don't want me to call the police. A coffee and a whisky.

(*The BARTENDER, cowed, goes grumbling back behind the bar. ESTELLE sits again on one of the barstools. JUAN, disconcerted, goes back to the cigarette machine and buys another pack. We hear the voices of the card players. RAMON comes through the door from the back room. He's a man about forty. In his undershirt. His face is flushed and wild looking. When he sees JUAN, he smiles. He goes up to him and starts talking in an urgent whisper.*)

RAMON: Juan, old buddy.
JUAN: How you doing?
RAMON: Bad. Can you lend me ten K, buddy?
JUAN: Ten thousand! Shit!
RAMON: You got your pension check today, didn't you?
JUAN: Yeah. But you owe me thirty already.
RAMON: Come on, Juanito. You got no family to feed.
JUAN: You going to take it home?
RAMON: I got to recoup me a little.
JUAN: No. Not interested.
RAMON: I can take him. The bastard. He can't get away from me now. How much you got?
JUAN: I got twenty-five left. But today's only. . . (*Doesn't remember.*) What's today?
RAMON: So lend me ten.
JUAN: Come on, Ramon, I can't. Not today. (*Looks at ESTELLE.*)
RAMON: Who's that?
JUAN: Shhh! Don't even look at her.
RAMON: Give me ten. I'll give you back fifteen in less than an hour. (*JUAN refuses.*) Twenty. (*JUAN shakes his head.*) Twenty-five, and you can come in on the game.
JUAN: No. I can't.
RAMON (*Aggressive*): Come on, Dominguez. Don't be a prick. You know if it wasn't for me, you'd never get in on a game.

(*ESTELLE turns toward the men.*)

JUAN (*Wanting to end the thing*): OK. (*Pulls out some money. A couple of bills fall to the floor. ESTELLE watches.*) Take it.
RAMON (*Giving him a few friendly pats on the shoulder*): Half an hour. I give it back, and I go home.
JUAN: Ramon, I think. . .
RAMON (*Leaves him with the words in his mouth and gestures to the BARTENDER.*): We're a little dry in there. (*He gives ESTELLE an impudent stare and then heads off to the back room.*)
BARTENDER (*To ESTELLE, setting them on the bar*): The coffee. The whisky.

(*JUAN goes over and punches up a record on the old jukebox. A love song, a bolero, starts to play. The BARTENDER grabs a tray and heads for the back* room. ESTELLE *writes something in her notebook. JUAN, with some trepidation, approaches her.)*

JUAN: Thanks, Estelle, honey. I knew you were a good kid.
ESTELLE: No. I'm not.
JUAN: But you deserve to be called a Torres, all right.
ESTELLE (*Handing him the whisky*): Here. I don't drink. This is for you.
JUAN: (*Feeling good.*) Deserve to be called Estelle. A star in the universe. "Star light, star bright, first star. . . " That's what your dad used to say. "Dominguez," he'd say, "I got three dark sons and one bright little star. Little but so bright."
ESTELLE: Is that what he'd say when he was sober or when he was drunk?
JUAN: I don't know. I don't see the difference.
ESTELLE: Right. There was no difference.
JUAN: Torres was always a good guy. Salt of the earth. And a card player. No one could touch him. Great card players are intelligent guys. Sometimes he would win; sometimes he would lose. But he was always a great card player.
ESTELLE: You used to win money from him? Or did the other guys get it out of him, like from you just now?
JUAN: What do you mean? Listen, Estelle. I'm sorry. Excuse me if I call you Estelle. It's just, you're little Estelle, the little girl–
ESTELLE: Yes, of course. Don't worry.
JUAN: "Don't worry." And please, call me Juan. Your father and I were very good friends.
ESTELLE: You weren't one of those who hit him up for money?
JUAN: Never. Torres was my close buddy, my partner. Whatever we won, we'd split.
ESTELLE: And then you'd throw it away on booze with some of your whores.
JUAN: You are a bad-mannered little girl.
ESTELLE: Why? It's true.
JUAN: Listen, little snot-nose. Certain lies are nice, and certain truths are just bad manners. I can see Torres didn't know how to bring you up. He should have smacked you more.
ESTELLE: You're right. Torres never touched me. Not to smack me, not to hug me, not even to put on my mittens in the winter. Torres only ever knew how to touch cards, money, and booze. Your friend Torres was a real disaster.
JUAN: You shouldn't talk like that about your own father.
ESTELLE: Is that a bad-mannered truth?
JUAN (*Upset*): You shouldn't talk like that about. . . someone who's dead.

(*There is a tense moment of silence. JUAN takes a drink. ESTELLE puts her hand to her brow.*)

ESTELLE: Dominguez. Give me a cigarette.
JUAN (*Pleased at this, he takes out three packs*): With filters? Without filters? Or black tobacco?
ESTELLE: With filters.

(*JUAN gives her one and takes one for himself. They both take out lighters at the same time. They look at each other. Then each lights up with his/her lighter.*)

JUAN: If he could see you now, he'd be very proud of you. Such a beautiful woman. And so important. I read your book. (*She looks at him, surprised.*) I did. I bought it. I saw you on TV, too, and in the papers.
ESTELLE: Did you like it?
JUAN: What?
ESTELLE: My novel.
JUAN: It choked me up. Every word, every comma, every period. But I don't know what it was about. I wasn't interested in the story. What I liked was that the book was by Torres's daughter. That's what got me. He never would have expected that from his little girl.
ESTELLE: Ah, but he was expecting something from somebody?
JUAN: Sure. He was hoping his boys would make something of themselves. Not like him. But turn out to be somebody important. Respected.
ESTELLE: Not like him.
JUAN: And his girl. . . that his girl would meet some nice man. Some man who wasn't like him.
ESTELLE: Yeah, well. We agree on that. I've spent my life looking for a man who wouldn't be like him.
JUAN: And did you find him?
ESTELLE (*After a pause*): No. Every man who's come into my life was like him one way or another.
JUAN (*Takes a drink.*): Torres was OK. He was. . . (*As he goes to set the glass down, he drops it.*)
ESTELLE (*Reacting angrily*): He was a phantom father, a weakling, a bad husband. A degenerate who sired children with his drunken sperm.
JUAN: That's not true!
ESTELLE: And you're just like him.
JUAN: Me, you can insult. But don't insult him. I won't let you. He was my best friend.
ESTELLE: And my shit father.
JUAN (*Hit hard by this*): You're an ungrateful and resentful daughter. You have no right to talk about him like that. (*Coughs.*) Poor man was sick. Talk about someone who. . . who. . . (*Loses his train of thought.*) He lived through the war. His head all messed up. (*Touches his head.*) Never went to school. They just threw us out on the streets. No school. You people. Never a pain, never afraid, never even a little hungry. You don't know what it's like to suffer. You don't know what it's like to be a man. To be a man with his head messed up. (*He can hardly get the words out.*) I'm going. (*Touching his chest.*) I've got a pain right here. (*Calling the BARTENDER.*) Hey, you! . . . Where is he?

(*The BARTENDER appears.*)

BARTENDER: Stop the shouting. What do you want?
JUAN: The check. (*Indicating ESTELLE's drink.*) Everything.
BARTENDER: You finally leaving?
ESTELLE: I'm not.
BARTENDER: I'm putting down the security door.
ESTELLE (*Pointing to the back room.*): So how do they get out?
BARTENDER: There's a back door for the card players.
JUAN: You better go now. What are you doing here anyway?

ESTELLE (*Perturbed.*): No. No, I can't. I have to make some more notes. I have to find out some things. They're still playing. I hear them. They're in there.
BARTENDER: Suit yourself. But I'm putting down the door.
JUAN (*Pointing to the front door*): Go out this way. Go on home now.
ESTELLE: I'm staying.
JUAN (*Shrugging his shoulders*): Well, goodbye then, Estelle.
ESTELLE: Goodbye.
JUAN: Here. Keep the filtered ones. (*She declines, shaking her head.*) I haven't touched them. I only bought them to offer you. (*He leaves the pack of cigarettes on the bar.*) Goodbye.

(*JUAN walks to the door. Just as he opens it, ESTELLE calls him. Her voice comes from deep inside her, like a call for help and sounding like an order.*)

ESTELLE: Dominguez! (*JUAN turns and looks at her.*) When my father didn't want to hear the truth. . . he'd walk out. (*Pause.*) Stay. Will you?

(*JUAN remains frozen where he is. Then, slowly, he comes back to her side.*)

BARTENDER (*Having had enough of it*): Suit yourself. (*He slams down the metal security door and goes off.*)
ESTELLE (*To JUAN, a painful memory*): One day. I couldn't have been more than seven or eight. I stood blocking the front door so he couldn't leave the house. He got angry. He said to me. "Get out of my way. Come on. Don't be stupid." I got down and grabbed his leg and held on with all my might. You know what he did? He pulled out a thousand peseta bill and waved it in front of me. "You want it?" he said. "For you." And I let go to grab it, and he slipped loose and walked past me. Just like that. By the time I figured it out, he was gone.
JUAN: Your dad was a generous guy. He wouldn't say no to anybody.
ESTELLE: Do you not understand because you're drunk or because you need more to drink? Tell me. What does it take for guys like you to comprehend something? What am I doing talking to a stiff?
JUAN: Now don't be like that. You're. . . you're hurt.
ESTELLE: No.
JUAN: You're shaking. (*Moves closer.*)
ESTELLE: Don't touch me!
JUAN: You're afraid.

(*ESTELLE, not knowing what to do, tries writing something in her notebook.*)

JUAN: You want a drink? I'll buy you one. Bartender!
ESTELLE: I told you I don't drink.
JUAN: To never drink alcohol is not. . . not good.

(*The BARTENDER, who has been going in and out of the back room, comes back in.*)

BARTENDER: What the hell d'you want now?
ESTELLE (*Forcefully*): Another whisky for the gentleman. (*The BARTENDER challenges her with a look.*) I said another whisky.

BARTENDER: Why don't you go somewhere else to tell the story of your life?
ESTELLE: It's OK. Just leave the bottle, and we won't bother you. How much is it?
BARTENDER (*After figuring it out*): Eight thousand pesetas. Bar price.
ESTELLE (*Giving him two five thousand notes*): Here.
JUAN: No. Not on your life. I can't let a woman pay for my drinks.
ESTELLE: With you, I'm not a woman.

(*JUAN looks at her in silence. The BARTENDER takes the bills from her.*)

ESTELLE: Keep the change, and don't bother us.

(*The BARTENDER leaves the bottle and goes out.*)

JUAN: You see. You're generous, too. Just like your father.
ESTELLE (*Laughing with a certain bitterness*): You're right. I can bribe people, too.
JUAN: You're so much like him. Your gestures. That laugh. The way you move your hands. In just that. . . way. You've got so much character. Just like him.
ESTELLE: Please. Don't say that.
JUAN: But it's true. It figures. What you see, you pick up.
ESTELLE: Then it's impossible that I'm like him. I was never with him. I hardly remember anything about him. He'd come home when I was asleep, and he'd leave when I was asleep.
JUAN: You were some sleeper.
ESTELLE: I was a little kid, Dominguez.
JUAN: And after that?
ESTELLE: After that he stopped coming home. I don't know who he was. He died five years ago, and I didn't have the remotest idea who he was.
JUAN: He was a good man.
ESTELLE: What else? Tell me something else. I need to know.
JUAN: He was. . . he was a great card player and a good friend.
ESTELLE: You've already told me that. Tell me some other things. Did he ever talk about me?
JUAN (*Thinks*): Yeah. Sometimes.
ESTELLE (*With some anxiety*): What did he say?
JUAN: Well. . . I don't know. I can't remember right now.
ESTELLE (*Pouring him some whisky*): Well, try. What did he tell you about me?
JUAN: He used to call you "his little star. First star. Star light, star bright."
ESTELLE: What else?
JUAN: And he used to say to me, "Juanito. I've got three dark sons and one bright little star."
ESTELLE: Why?
JUAN: I don't know. Maybe it was your red hair. Or maybe not? Yeah, he liked your hair. Or maybe it's me who likes your hair?
ESTELLE: Before you said you remembered my look, a lost look mixed with. . . (*She doesn't remember.*)
JUAN: Insolence. Insolence.
ESTELLE: You knew me when I was little? How was that? Was I with my father?
JUAN (*Doubtful*): No. No, you weren't with Torres.

ESTELLE: Then, how was it? Try to remember.
JUAN (*Trying to remember*): One night your mother and you came in looking for him. Here.
ESTELLE: Here?
JUAN: Or was it the club?
ESTELLE: Think hard.
JUAN: I don't remember which.
ESTELLE: Please.
JUAN: Yeah. It was here. Yeah. I'm sure it was here. (*ESTELLE gets up and looks around the bar trying to remember it.*) Your mother just appeared. Dark hair. Very beautiful. One classy woman. She came in looking for Torres. You were in her arms. You couldn't have been more than three. But you had those eyes and that look of insolence. Your mother was crying, and she was yelling at your father, and you. . . You were watching them. Her and him. With that look.
ESTELLE: That's not insolence, Dominguez. That's terror.
JUAN: Your father was saying, "You didn't have to drag the kid in here." And your mother, says, "If you were at home, we wouldn't have to come looking for you."
ESTELLE: Here? I've been in this place before.
JUAN: And you were taking it all in. Just like tonight. Torres told your mother. "Go on home. I'll be there in a while."
ESTELLE: What a good-for-nothing!
JUAN: He was winning big. He couldn't pull out of the game. You're not allowed. Your father was a great card player.
ESTELLE: A great son-of-a-bitch. That's what he was. I mean, he couldn't pull himself away from that scum losing their money, but he could send his wife and kid home alone at that hour of the night. His half-desperate wife, while he. . . What a louse!

(*ESTELLE opens her bag and takes out some coins. She starts compulsively to feed them into the slot machine. Finally amidst angry outbursts she starts beating on the machine. She hits it harder and harder. JUAN watches her with alarm. He pours some whisky in her coffee cup and takes it to her.*)

JUAN: Don't get so upset. That was a long time ago. Why bring it all back now?
ESTELLE: Leave me alone!

(*The BARTENDER comes in.*)

BARTENDER: What's going on out here?

(*ESTELLE deliberately ignores him.*)

JUAN: Nothing's going on.
BARTENDER: The woman is crazy. Lady!
JUAN: Just leave her alone. She's a little upset.
BARTENDER: Lady, you're going to bust the machine.

(*ESTELLE stops hitting the machine but continues to put in coins.*)

First Star - 13

JUAN (*To the BARTENDER*): You see. Nothing's going on. That's it. Problem solved. (*A voice is heard from the back room.*) They're calling you.

(*The BARTENDER, still watching ESTELLE, fills his tray and goes out.*)

JUAN: You know how to play poker? (*She doesn't hear him. He raises his voice.*) D'you play poker?
ESTELLE: No. No. No. God, no! I've never played poker in my life!
JUAN: Well, it's in your blood. You'd be a great poker player.
ESTELLE (*Not listening to him*): Do you have any change?
JUAN (*Pulling some out of his pocket*): Here.

(*ESTELLE, somewhat calmer, continues to feed the machine.*)

JUAN: Me, now, I'm no friend of the machines. I mean, sometimes I feed 'em a little change. (*Pointing to the other room.*) They don't like me in on their game. They only let me play when there's no one else. My memory's slippin' and, (*Touching the machine.*) These things are only good for lonely women and wasted old men.

(*ESTELLE runs out of change.*)

ESTELLE (*Anxiously*): You have any more change? It's ready to sing.
JUAN: Come on. Let it go. It always seems like it's ready, but it never gets there.
ESTELLE (*Dumping her bag*): Shit! Tell him to come here and give me some change. Go on, get him. Please.
JUAN: Hey, hey, hey. Take it easy now. You're all upset. (*Mysteriously coming up with a coin.*) Here. The last one.

(*ESTELLE puts it in. The machine starts to play its little pay-off tune.*)

ESTELLE: Did you see that?
JUAN: How lucky can you get! I forgot. You're a Torres.

(*The money starts falling in a rush. ESTELLE gathers it up and gives half to JUAN.*)

ESTELLE: Here. Take it. This is yours.
JUAN: No, no. Don't even suggest it.
ESTELLE: Don't be silly. The coin was yours. Now take it.
JUAN (*A matter of dignity*): No. I said no.
ESTELLE: Whatever you say. (*Takes the coins and starts putting them in the machine again.*)
JUAN: Well, if you're going to throw it away, then give me my share.
ESTELLE (*Giving him some*): Here. Your share.
JUAN (*Smiling and enjoying the situation*): It's like being back with Torres again. (*He starts towards her to give her a pat with his hand. She backs away from him. Depressed suddenly, she sits at a table.*)

(*JUAN goes over to the jukebox.*)

JUAN: Listen, I'm going to put on a song. Something easy to calm the jitters. Something your dad used to like a lot, too. (*He laughs.*) He knew the words. Used to sing it pretty well. Listen. Torres.

(*The same bolero as before starts playing. JUAN starts to hum along. Then he gets more into it and starts singing. He picks up the bottle and dances with it as if it were his woman. ESTELLE watches him with a look which is a mix of sad, angry, and puzzled. JUAN finishes up the bolero singing to ESTELLE. Then he goes over to her and hands her the cup with the whisky in it.*)

JUAN: Here. This is good. Take a sip.
ESTELLE (*Shakes her head "no." Then looks at JUAN firmly*): Tell me. Who are you?
JUAN: A man. (*Pause.*) An old man. And you?
ESTELLE: I guess I have to answer a woman. A woman, still young. Right?
JUAN: That I can see. Young, beautiful, and successful. But that's not what I want to know.
ESTELLE: And what do you want to know?
JUAN: Are you married? You have children?
ESTELLE: Married? No. Well, I lived with a man for a while, and we had a baby. (*Smiles and her face lights up.*) And now I have a wonderful son. . . (*Serious again.*) But I don't have a man.
JUAN: You separated?
ESTELLE: Yeah. We didn't understand each other. (*Pause.*) I mean, it was really me. I never, I never know what to do with a man in the house.
JUAN: With a man, you don't have to do anything.
ESTELLE: If you don't do anything, they leave.
JUAN: But we always come back. If you leave the door open for us. If we know you're waiting for us, we come back.
ESTELLE: No. I don't know how to wait. I need them to wait for me.
JUAN: Now that's bad business, kid. That's something we men don't know how to do.
ESTELLE (*From deep inside her*): Why? Why not?
JUAN: Because we're made to be out there on the move. We don't know how to stay still. Understand? And to be able to wait you got to know how to sit still.
ESTELLE: A shame, isn't it? I have to be on the move, too. My life is out there on the street. My novels take place on the street. I find my characters on the street. I have to get out there and sell my books on the street. (*Her deepest feeling.*) A shame, isn't it? A real shame that they never know how to wait for me.
JUAN: So, you still love him?
ESTELLE: Who?
JUAN: Your son's father.
ESTELLE: No. No way. (*Thinking about it.*) I don't think I ever loved him.
JUAN: Don't talk crazy. You're not the type that sleeps with just anybody.
ESTELLE (*Smiling at his not understanding*): No. No, you don't understand. I didn't know I didn't love him till after, when it was too late to do anything about it. (*Pause.*) That's when I find out they didn't love me either.
JUAN: Don't talk nonsense. A woman like you must have hundreds of men at her feet. Young guys today are stupid jerks. If I was twenty years younger, I wouldn't let you get away.

ESTELLE: You. . . you don't know. You don't know what I'm like. I'm not some sweet thing. And I don't want to be.
JUAN: The sweetest candies are the ones that come wrapped up the nicest. But you got to know how to unwrap that silver foil without damaging the goods.
ESTELLE (*Gives JUAN a tender look, but then suddenly turns defensive*): Words. Everyone's world is full of words. I know how to play with them, too. You bet. And most of the men in my life knew how. But still, none of them knew how to unwrap the silver foil, and the candy got stale. So now, here we are, an old man and a woman. . . (*Touching her heart.*) Who's old. (*She picks up the cup with whisky and takes a drink.*)
JUAN (*Angry with her*): You don't know what you're talking about. You're still being the spoiled little girl. Ungrateful. (*Looking at her, nodding agreement.*) Yeah, but you're right. You do look old. You're wearing the terrible look of an old woman.
ESTELLE: You have no right to talk to me like that. I. . . I. . .
JUAN: But when you smile. When you smile and let your eyes light up. Come on, smile, Estelle!
ESTELLE: What for? I don't feel like smiling.
JUAN: Smile without feeling like it. Come on, try.
ESTELLE: What for?
JUAN: Just do it a minute. Before, when you told me about your son, you did it real well. (*ESTELLE takes a deep breath and sighs.*) Smile, damn it.
ESTELLE (*Forces a smile. Then really smiles*): You're crazy. You're completely nutty.
JUAN: There you go. And now you're a young woman, with a sparkle in your eyes, with a future. Now, look at me. What do you see in my face?
ESTELLE (*Disconcerted*): I don't know.
JUAN: Of course you know. Say it. Don't be afraid. Say it.
ESTELLE (*Looking at him carefully*): I see wrinkles. A map full of crisscrossed wrinkles. Roads surrounded by blotches. And yellow, a yellowish tone deep in your eyes. . .
JUAN: OK. And now I'll smile. (*Smiles.*) And now what do you see?
ESTELLE: I don't understand.
JUAN: You still see a face full of wrinkles and blotches, and the same yellow eyes. You understand the difference between us? That's the difference.

(*ESTELLE remains silent. She takes a cigarette from JUAN's pack and lights it.*)

ESTELLE: Do you have a wife?
JUAN: What?
ESTELLE: I asked if you have a wife?
JUAN: No. She died. Nine years ago. (*Pause.*) She had an illness called Juan Dominguez. It's a kind of slow-killing virus. The last stage is one of hate, and the hate leads to death. It was a slow death. Took thirty years.
ESTELLE: Why didn't you do anything to prevent it?
JUAN: Like what? I didn't know what to do. Besides, she didn't want to be cured.
ESTELLE: Maybe she loved you.
JUAN: Loved me? Yeah, she must have loved me. We loved each other, for a time. And, at times, we even used to make love. We had two children, both of them

ashamed of me. They never come to see me. They're sick, too. She transmitted her illness to them: Juan Dominguez.
ESTELLE: You're dangerous.
JUAN (*Laughs*): Dangerous? Me? Hell, I've never even been able to kill a fly. I mean, it's not that I like flies. It's just, I think, you know, live and let live.
ESTELLE (*Taking another swallow of her drink*): Now me, I hate flies, and I kill them. They're clumsy and stupid. And they can get into people's ears by mistake and buzz around. I grab the spray, and *zap*, I blow them away.
JUAN (*Laughing*): They get in your ears?
ESTELLE: When they crawl into your ears, they die in there. They can't find their way out. The canal closes up, and they get stuck in the wax like it was honey. But it's earwax, not honey. Disgusting bugs! And when a rainstorm comes up they go crazy and walk around all over your body like it was their place. No, they're not aggressive; they're stupid, and they love shit.
JUAN: I like your sense of humor. I like a person you can talk with about anything.
ESTELLE (*Laughing*): Yes. Great conversation. I think the one going crazy is me.
JUAN (*Laughing ingenuously*): Philosophy. That's philosophy, sweetheart.

(*The sound of footsteps. RAMON, all worked up, enters from the back room.*)

RAMON: Juan, Juanito. . . (*Looks at ESTELLE.*) Sorry, you. . . ah. . .
JUAN: This is Martita, my. . . daughter.
RAMON (*Surprised)*: Oh. Nice to meet you.
ESTELLE (*Hesitates. Then answers*): Hello.
RAMON (*To JUAN*): Can you come here for a minute?
JUAN: Yeah. Sure. (*To ESTELLE.*) Excuse me, honey.

(*JUAN and RAMON go off to one side. We hear their urgent conversation.*)

RAMON: You got to let me have five more.
JUAN: I can't, Ramon. That doesn't leave me enough to get home.
RAMON: I need it, Juan. God damn it! Shit! My luck's gotta change.
JUAN: Pull out now. Go on home.
RAMON: I can't now. Lemme have ten more, and you can play the last round. Pastor's already broke. He'll take off in a bit. Just lend me enough to recoup, and you play the last game. You got my word.
JUAN (*Unbending*): I can't. I've got to go with my daughter.
RAMON: I didn't know you–
JUAN: She came looking for me. (*With pride.*) Had to talk to me about a family matter. Something urgent.
RAMON: She's good-looking.
JUAN (*Obviously already taken by her*): Very.
RAMON: Come on, Juan. Lend me something.
JUAN (*Looking at ESTELLE, caught up by her*): Very good looking. Take it. (*He takes out his wallet and hands him some bills without taking his eyes off ESTELLE.*) Very good looking.
RAMON (*A big show of thanks to JUAN*): I'll let you know when Pastor takes off, OK? (*He takes off quickly to the back room.*)

(JUAN *comes out of his daze and, to his surprise, discovers his hand empty. ESTELLE's face takes on an angry look again. JUAN goes back to ESTELLE's table.*)

JUAN: He's a good friend. Great card player.
ESTELLE: Yeah. Another phoney who's not ashamed to take your money. I can't deal with that kind of trash. Look, I better go.
JUAN: You're going? You can't go yet. Let me introduce you to the rest of them.
ESTELLE: Are you crazy? I'm not your daughter.
JUAN: What does it matter for one night? It'll only take a minute. D'you see how impressed Ramon was? If they met you, they'd show me a little respect again. They'd know I'm not just some guy whose luck's run out, that I've got family, too.
ESTELLE: That would be another one of your lies. You'd be showing off a daughter who wasn't your daughter, and who doesn't love you.
JUAN (*Without hurt, just trying to convince her*): Doesn't matter. My daughter doesn't love me either.
ESTELLE: No, Dominguez. I'm not going to play that game. I'm really tired. And I didn't come here to save somebody's life.
JUAN: So, why did you come here?
ESTELLE (*Not finding the reply*): I don't know. But I'm going now.
JUAN: Please. Come on in with me. It'll take two minutes. Just so they see us together. So they see how good looking you are and. . . how you take after me.
ESTELLE: Dominguez! I think you've got the D. T.'s.
JUAN: Please, Estelle. Honey. I'm old. My head's messed up. Can't you understand that?
ESTELLE: No, I can't understand that. I look at you. I listen to you. But, I can't figure out who you are. I see that dirty mask. It's unreal. And it hurts me. So much.
JUAN: I wasn't always like this. Don't think I was always like this. I was young. I was good looking. I had tons of women after me. I was a guy with a future. (*Pause.*) I was intelligent, too. I started off pushing a wheelbarrow and ended up being a head bookkeeper. Yeah, I wrote books, too, like you. Only account books. Numbers, thousands of numbers, all set down in their right places. Numbers on the left, numbers on the right, numbers on the left, numbers–
ESTELLE (*Interrupting him*): I'm really tired. I've been drinking, and I'm not used to it. I want to get out of here.
JUAN: You got to listen to me first. You can't leave until you listen to me!
ESTELLE: Drunks never tell the truth.
JUAN: I'm not drunk! I know perfectly what I'm saying. Besides, people are more than just words, aren't we?
ESTELLE (*Half in a daze*): I don't know.
JUAN: I'm a person. You're a person.
ESTELLE: I don't know anything.
JUAN: What I'm trying to say is that I knew how to love, too. And I still have a heart, damn it. And a mouth and hands. And I. . . (*Truthfully.*) And I love you. A lot. (*ESTELLE doesn't react. Moved, she lowers her head.*) That rebellious hair. That red hair. (*He starts to touch it.*)
ESTELLE (*Pulling back*): The only thing my father liked about me.

JUAN: Not the only thing. It's what he liked most about you. (*Pause.*) Your mother had gorgeous hair, too. I fell in love with her the moment I saw her. God. It was unbelievable, first time I met her. And then, hot soups, darned socks, and breasts. Soft breasts where I would lay my head. God, yes. I was in love.

ESTELLE: But you were never at home. Were you?

JUAN: That was later. Years after we got married. I stopped moving up in the business. I must have started losing it. My messed-up head. Fuses blown.

ESTELLE: Drinking. Drinking.

JUAN: I was never bringing in enough for all her little whims. And she would scold me. Fuss at me about everything. Deny me her breasts. (*Pause.*) She would talk and talk and talk, and I. . . said nothing. Stock still before the goddess, before the victim. Coming home at night and opening the door was like walking into a tiger's cage.

ESTELLE (*Aggressive*): Opening the cage door at three, or four, or five, or six in the morning. Or the next day.

JUAN: Scratching me, biting me, hitting me. No mercy. You don't know how afraid of her I was.

ESTELLE (*Full of anger*): And then you would take off, running like a coward and hide out in this horrible place while she went on with her sweeping and washing and sewing and suffering. She raised us kids by herself. That was home for me. A house with no man. God, what nights! All those nights I spent praying you'd get home early so we wouldn't hear the yelling! How can someone be so cruel and irresponsible?

JUAN: I never laid a hand on you. Never!

ESTELLE: I didn't say you did. You tortured me in more subtle ways.

JUAN: But me. Oh, yeah. My old man beat me with his belt and with his fists. He'd call me a puny little shit. He couldn't stand it that I was small and weak. When I was twelve he brought me to Madrid and threw me out on my own. With my head. Look. (*He pulls back his hair and shows ESTELLE an enormous scar.*)

ESTELLE (*Startled*): What is that?

JUAN: My head busted from top to bottom.

ESTELLE: Who did that to you?

JUAN: It doesn't matter.

ESTELLE: Did your father do that to you?

JUAN (*Bitterly*): Yes. Because he sent me off to war. I didn't want to go. I was still a kid. (*He goes silent.*)

ESTELLE: And what happened?

JUAN: I don't think anyone gave a damn about me. They left me alone on a cot. Unconscious. And one day, I woke up.

ESTELLE: But how did it happen?

JUAN (*Unsure*): I, I was part of a forward patrol. An enemy tank column was closing on our position. You could hear artillery in the distance. . . Boom. . . Boom. . . Boom!

ESTELLE (*Interrupting him*): You're lying.

JUAN: Am I? Really?

ESTELLE: Why? Why are you always lying?

JUAN: I don't realize I am. (*Pause.*) My head. Who did hit me? I'm sorry. I'm. . . old. Sorry, sweetheart.

ESTELLE: You can't have forgotten that!
JUAN (*Thinking*): My head, my head. Yeah. Sure. (*Pause.*) If I tell you the truth, you won't tell anyone?
ESTELLE: No.
JUAN: In my village. A mule... kicked me.
ESTELLE (*Can't keep from laughing*): That's terrible!
JUAN: Yeah. You know, I used to like watching him. And your flies. They really did their job on him. And he would just stand there and wag his ears like there was no tomorrow. That's where I learned to do it. You remember? (*Simpatico.*) Look! It used to fascinate you when you were little.

(*JUAN concentrates and wiggles his ears.*)

ESTELLE: Hey! You can really move them! (*Laughs.*) Looks like you're about to take off.
JUAN: And what do you think of this? (*He starts making faces, each one uglier than the last. ESTELLE is laughing.*) Look at this. Hey, and this, huh?
ESTELLE (*Like a child now*): Too ugly.
JUAN: Well, look at this.
ESTELLE (*Enjoying it*): Yikes, come on! That's spooky.
JUAN: See, you're having fun. You're laughing. I'm pappy, the ugliest man in the world. Pappy Boo Boo, pappy bear. (*Starts talking like Yogi Bear.*) Hey, Boo Boo, let's catch this bad little girl and throw her in the clink. (*Imitating Boo Boo.*) You mean it, Yogi? You bet, Boo Boo. This little redheaded girl is beginning to bug me. Look at her. She's laughing at me. She's laughing at me!

(*JUAN starts chasing ESTELLE, who runs away, enjoying it, trying not to get caught. The BARTENDER, who has entered, watches, confused by what is going on. JUAN and ESTELLE, suddenly realizing the BARTENDER is there, stop dead in their tracks.*)

BARTENDER: Are you two for real or what? Can't you go out in the street to do your clown act?
JUAN (*With his Yogi Bear voice*): Look, little girl. What a dumb doggie-doo who got lost in the park.
BARTENDER: I'll give you fucking lost in the park.
JUAN (*Sticking with the game*): Oh, I don't think so. You're a little, midget Chihuahua and I can flatten you with a smack of my paw. (*Makes growling bear sounds.*)
BARTENDER: You're a big, brave fellow in front of the lady here. I don't know who she might be, but–
JUAN: Tell him, lady.

(*The BARTENDER looks at ESTELLE; she lets out a loud bark at him. He is dumbstruck. JUAN and ESTELLE confront him, growling and barking with increasing gusto. The BARTENDER finally makes a dismissive gesture and goes off. ESTELLE cheers. They applaud and laugh.*)

JUAN: Now, give me your hand.
ESTELLE (*She stops playing*): What for?

JUAN: Come on. I'm going to show you a magic trick.
ESTELLE (*Frightened*): No. Don't.
JUAN: Don't be silly. (*Holding his hand out.*) Come on. I'm not going to cut it off.

(*ESTELLE holds her hand out. JUAN goes to take it, but she pulls back.*)

ESTELLE: No. I can't. I can't touch you.
JUAN (*After a moment*): Oh, yeah. I disgust you. I forgot.
ESTELLE: No. I don't know what it is, but–
JUAN (*Crestfallen*): I can go wash my hands.
ESTELLE: No. No.
JUAN: I mean, I'm clean. I wash up every morning. And I put on cologne. You don't believe me? I'm an old fool, but I'm a clean one.
ESTELLE: Of course you are. I know that.
JUAN: Tobacco, booze, and age. All leave dirt. They all leave us dirty inside and out. (*Rubs his yellowed fingers together.*) See? It won't come off. It's in the skin.
ESTELLE: Don't say that. You don't disgust me. It's just... Well, I'm not used to it. He... You... He never touched me.
JUAN: That's not true. What's happened is you don't remember.
ESTELLE: No. I don't remember.
JUAN (*Coming closer to her*): Look, I would hold your hands, and you–
ESTELLE (*Repulsed*): Don't get so close! Don't touch me! I can't stand it. For drunks to touch me.

(*JUAN is stopped dead by this. ESTELLE also. They look at each other in silence.*)

JUAN (*His mind made up*): You wait here. I'll be right back.

(*He heads out to the lavatory. ESTELLE doesn't know what to do. Then she automatically goes over to the slot machine. RAMON enters, now relaxed and all smiles.*)

RAMON: Where is your... dad?
ESTELLE: What do you want?
RAMON: Want to talk to him.
ESTELLE: You going to give him back his money?
RAMON: Where is he?
ESTELLE: He went to the men's room, but you can give the money to me.
RAMON: When he comes back, tell him to step inside a minute.
ESTELLE: Step inside, for what?
RAMON: That's not your business, beautiful.
ESTELLE: Give me back the money you got from him. You're despicable. You take advantage of him because he's old and–
RAMON: And you, what about you? Heh?
ESTELLE: What are you insinuating?
RAMON: Come on. You think I'm still wet behind the ears? He's not your old man.
ESTELLE: Yes he is.

RAMON: Right. And what? You're out having a couple drinks together?
ESTELLE: What my father and I do is none of your business.
RAMON: Meaning, you know when he gets his pension check in the mail, too?
ESTELLE: What are you saying?
RAMON: This is not a place where nice women hang out.
ESTELLE (*Contemptuously*): That's obvious. (*She turns her back on him.*)
RAMON (*Getting too close to her):* You're too good looking to come down this low. (*He grabs her by the waist.*)
ESTELLE (*She turns to try and slap him*): And you're a scum-pig.
RAMON (*Grabbing her by the wrists)*: You're crazy.
ESTELLE (*Trying to break free*): Give him back his money! Give it back, pig!
RAMON: Quiet!
ESTELLE: You drunk! Degenerate!

(*RAMON pushes her backwards and throws a handful of bills at her.*)

RAMON: Take it. Tell the old man he can come in and play.

(*RAMON goes out. ESTELLE picks up the money and puts it on the table. She takes the whisky bottle and pours herself some in the cup. She is rattled. JUAN comes back in. He is washed up and has his hair combed. She looks at him and smiles.*)

JUAN: What do you think?
ESTELLE: I think. . . you're very handsome.
JUAN: I washed my face and hands with soap. I'm a new man.
ESTELLE: Yes. (*Giving him the money.*) Here. That man brought these in.
JUAN: Ah, Ramon. Lucky. He recouped. A real friend.
ESTELLE (*Still scared*): He said you can come in and play.
JUAN (*Happy about this*): He did? (*He looks towards the back room. Then at ESTELLE.*) No. I don't think I'll play now. First I want to do my magic trick for you. (*Pause.*) Will you give me your hand?

(*ESTELLE looks at him. She is frightened.*)

JUAN: It's real easy, honey. I'll hardly touch your skin. Give me your hand.
ESTELLE (*Slowly reaching out her trembling hands*): Like this?
JUAN (*He takes a small red ball out of his pocket*): Look at this. I always carry it in my pocket to have a little fun with the kids on my block. They're nice kids, and they get a kick out of it. They try to figure out the trick, looking up my sleeves, in my pockets. But they never find the little ball. Instead there's always some candy or a coin. I like the kids because they never ask who the hell I am. I like them even though I know they take the candy and run. (*He places the ball on the table.*) Now, pick it up and put it on my hand. (*ESTELLE slowly does so.*) Now, I close my hand, and you sprinkle it with magic dust. (*She shyly makes the gesture.*) OK. That's good. Now say, "Magic ball, pass from his hand to my heart."
ESTELLE: Magic ball, pass from his hand to my heart.
JUAN: Abracadabra. . . (*He opens his hand.*) The little ball has disappeared!
ESTELLE: Where is it?

JUAN: Ahhh. I don't know. Look for it.
ESTELLE: It's in your pocket.
JUAN (*Turning his pockets out*): Nope.
ESTELLE: Up your sleeve.
JUAN (*Pushing up his sleeves*): No, little lady, it's not. Now, give me your hand. (*With real authority.*) Give it to me. (*ESTELLE holds her hand out. JUAN shows his empty one.*) You see. Nothing in my hand.

(*JUAN places his hand over hers and begins to touch her very carefully. It is a long and tense moment. ESTELLE closes her eyes, moved by this.*)

JUAN: You see how easy it is? (*With great delicacy.*) You rub a little here. You rub a little there. Close your hand. (*She does. He continues touching her closed hand.*) And we say, "Little lost ball that's gone astray, to a little girl's hand now find your way." Abracadabra! Open your hand. (*The ball is in ESTELLE's hand.*)
ESTELLE (*With child-like fascination*): How did you do that?
JUAN: Aha! Magician's secret.
ESTELLE: Your hand is so soft.
JUAN: And now the little red ball will turn into–
ESTELLE (*Interrupting*): Give me. Give me your hand again. (*ESTELLE takes JUAN's hand and touches his fingers.*) It's soft. It's very soft. It's good, and it's trembling. . .
JUAN (*Pulling back his hand*): And now the silly magician is going to pull a bird out of the pretty little lady's head. Out of this head with the most rebellious hair in the world.
ESTELLE: No.
JUAN: You don't want me to take out all the birds? (*She shakes her head.*) What about a handkerchief as white as a dove?
ESTELLE: No.
JUAN (*Getting nervous*): Let's see. Let's see. A scarf with lots of colors?
ESTELLE: No.
JUAN: A broken comb?
ESTELLE: No.
JUAN (*More nervous*): A big bill worth thousands of pesetas? (*She shakes her head.*) Then, what does the little lady want?
ESTELLE (*Looking him in the eyes*): I want you to touch me. Touch me gently.

(*After a moment's pause, JUAN begins to caress her hair. He is very moved. ESTELLE hides her head in his hands.*)

JUAN: I want to tell you. . . I want you to know. . .
ESTELLE: Shhh. Don't say anything. Keep touching me.

(*JUAN continues to caress her with great tenderness.*)

ESTELLE: Just tell me what you're feeling.
JUAN: I. . . I don't know. . . I don't know how to explain it.
ESTELLE: Do you like it?
JUAN: Oh yes. Very much. I feel. . .

First Star - 23

ESTELLE: What do you feel, Daddy?
JUAN: I feel. . . I'm a person.
ESTELLE: You are a person, an important person. You're good. You're a good man.
JUAN: I'm damaged goods, darling. A mental retard. I've spent my life. . . lost in this nowhere place. Never could pull myself away from here. Stuck, like all the other cowards. I. . . I want to ask you to forgive me.
ESTELLE (*With infinite strength*): Oh, yes. I forgive you. I forgive you.
JUAN: I like to hear that. It's the first time anyone's said that to me: I forgive you.
ESTELLE: Poor darling. . . poor baby. . . (*She caresses him as if he were a child.*) So little. So all alone. My poor darling. My Daddy Rafael. My Rafi. My little Rafi.

(*When JUAN hears the name, he pulls away, overcome with emotion. He reacts with new energy.*)

JUAN: Rafael. Rafael Torres! It's very hard, failure. Some can't survive it, Estelle. And they die.
ESTELLE: But not you. You're not going to die.
JUAN: Rafael Torres, your father, couldn't deal with it. I saw him, shaking. Pounding his fists against the wall. . .
ESTELLE (*Confused*): What? What are you saying?
JUAN: That I saw your father crying.
ESTELLE: My father? Why?
JUAN: Because his little girl, Estelle, called him a dirty bastard.

(*ESTELLE clutches her belly as if she's just been hit.*)

JUAN: Torres was weak, and he made mistakes, but he had feelings. His heart was shriveled but full of pain. (*His voice breaking.*) And he had one friend: Juan Dominguez. And a messed-up head.
ESTELLE: My poor Daddy.
JUAN: He got taken in by this lie of a life. It plays its trick with us. But you're young, and you can still beat it, and be happy. You hear me? Your father wanted to beat it, but he knew it was impossible. For him, from the start, it was impossible. And then he ran out of time. His liver went bad. He kept drinking. With a sick liver and no winning hands. . . you lose your will. . .
ESTELLE: My poor Daddy.
JUAN: I've seen him pounding his fists against the wall because his little girl called him a dirty bastard. . .
ESTELLE: You said that already! It's true. But he hurt me, too. He was never there and I blamed myself for having a father like that. And I'm not to blame. It's not my fault, his pounding the wall, his sick liver. The kick in the head, the shit, the whisky. . . (*With a heartrending scream.*) It's not my fault. (*She breaks out crying.*)
JUAN: Of course it's not, honey. You're the only bright star who's come out tonight. (*Opening his arms to her.*) "Star light, star bright, first star. . ."

(*ESTELLE hugs him. RAMON enters and surprises them embracing.*)

RAMON: Well, catch the old man. Not as dumb as he looks.

(*JUAN and ESTELLE do not look at him.*)

RAMON (*Getting their attention*): Pastor's taken off. You want in on the last game?
ESTELLE: We're going, too.
RAMON: Right.
ESTELLE: This one's leaving and he's not coming back.
RAMON: Well, OK (*Turns to go.*)
JUAN: Ramon. (*RAMON turns.*) How goes it?
RAMON (*Nod of understanding. Takes out some bills*): Here. We're even.
JUAN: I'll be right in.
RAMON: Make it fast. (*Goes off.*)
ESTELLE (*Incredulous*): You're going in there?
JUAN: Yeah. I made a deal with my friend.
ESTELLE: A deal? Your friend? He's not your friend. The guy's using you.
JUAN: Easy. You can't understand it. But Ramon is a friend.
ESTELLE: This guy is some leech and this place is a filthy cesspool. Let's get out of here.
JUAN: I can't, Estelle. They need me to keep the game going. You understand that?
ESTELLE: You've got to leave this. Don't go in there, please. Let's get out of here.
JUAN (*Very composed*): Get out of here? To where?
ESTELLE: To. . . To. . . (*She can't find an answer. She goes silent. Then she nods her head, agreeing, recognizing the truth, accepting. She smiles and looks at JUAN.*)
JUAN: You go, Estelle. And don't even think of coming back here. (*She nods, agreeing. A soft, relaxed smile forms on her face.*) Don't even think of coming back here. You understand me?
ESTELLE (*Convinced and transformed*): Yes.

(*RAMON comes in with the BARTENDER.*)

RAMON: Are you coming in or not, Dominguez?
JUAN: Yeah! One minute! (*ESTELLE gathers her things and starts toward the back room.*) Where are you going?
ESTELLE: This door's locked.
JUAN: Well, it'll open. (*To BARTENDER.*) You, open the door.
BARTENDER: Let her go out the back.
JUAN: She's going out the front if it's the last thing I do.
ESTELLE: Forget it. It doesn't matter.
JUAN: Shhh! You, always by the front door and with your head high. Understood? (*ESTELLE nods agreement, happily.*) What did I say?
ESTELLE: Me, always by the front door and with my head high.
JUAN (*To the BARTENDER*): Give me the keys.
RAMON: Give him the keys, idiot. They're waiting for us.

(*The BARTENDER starts for the door. JUAN sticks his hand out and stops him.*)

JUAN: I don't need your help. I think I still got what it takes to open a door.

(*The BARTENDER throws him the keys. JUAN catches them, unlocks, and, drawing strength from somewhere, manages to raise the heavy, metal security door.*)

JUAN (*To ESTELLE, stepping aside for her*): Goodbye.

(*ESTELLE starts out. Suddenly she turns.*)

ESTELLE (*In a loud, firm voice*): Father. . . (*The three men look at her.*)
JUAN: Huh?
ESTELLE: Daddy. I love you.

(*JUAN doesn't know what to say. He looks at the two men.*)

JUAN: I know that, honey. I know that.
ESTELLE (*To the two men*): Good night. Good night. All of you. (*She exits.*)

(*JUAN pulls down the door with surprising force. RAMON and the BARTENDER exchange a glance.*)

JUAN (*To RAMON*): My shining star. First star. My Martita. Right, Ramon? (*RAMON shrugs his shoulders, still confused. To the BARTENDER.*) Whisky, friend! Whisky for everyone! Tonight the drinks are on me.

(*RAMON goes into the back room staggering. JUAN follows him. The lights come down to black.*)

CURTAIN

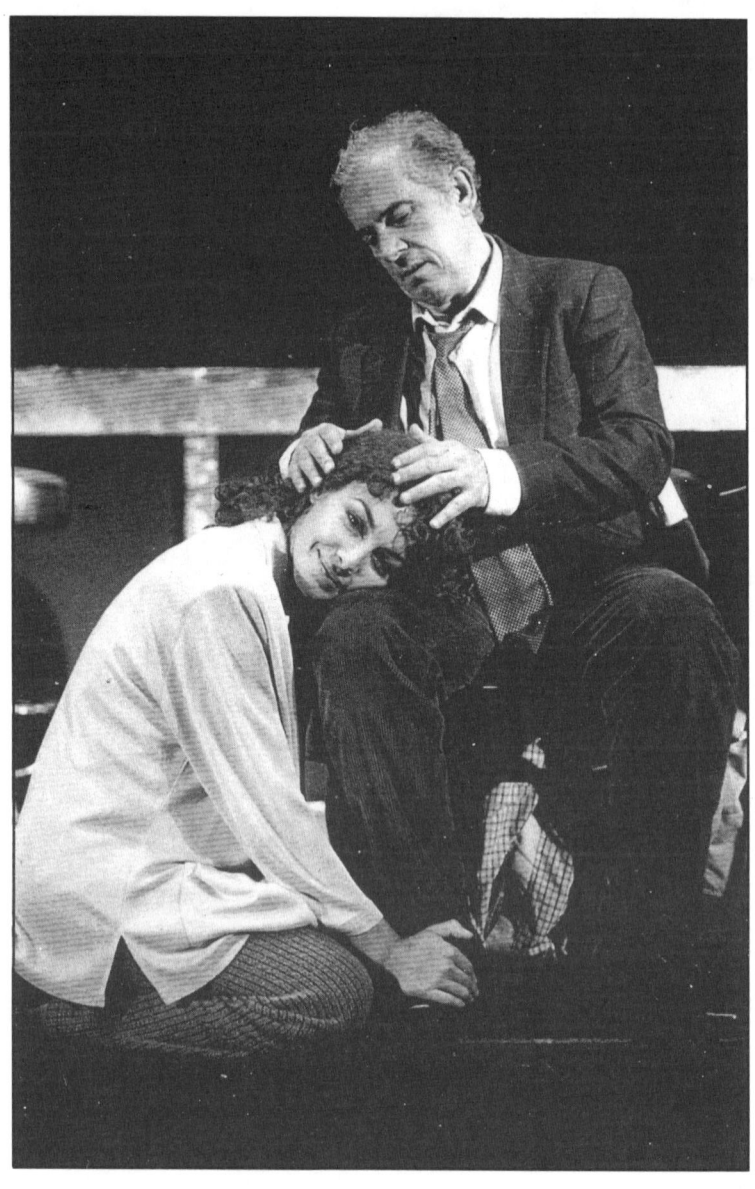

Mapi Galán and Pancho García in *Una estrella (First Star)*. Madrid, 1999.
Directed by Panchika Velez and Paloma Pedrero.
Photo courtesy of producer Robert Muro.

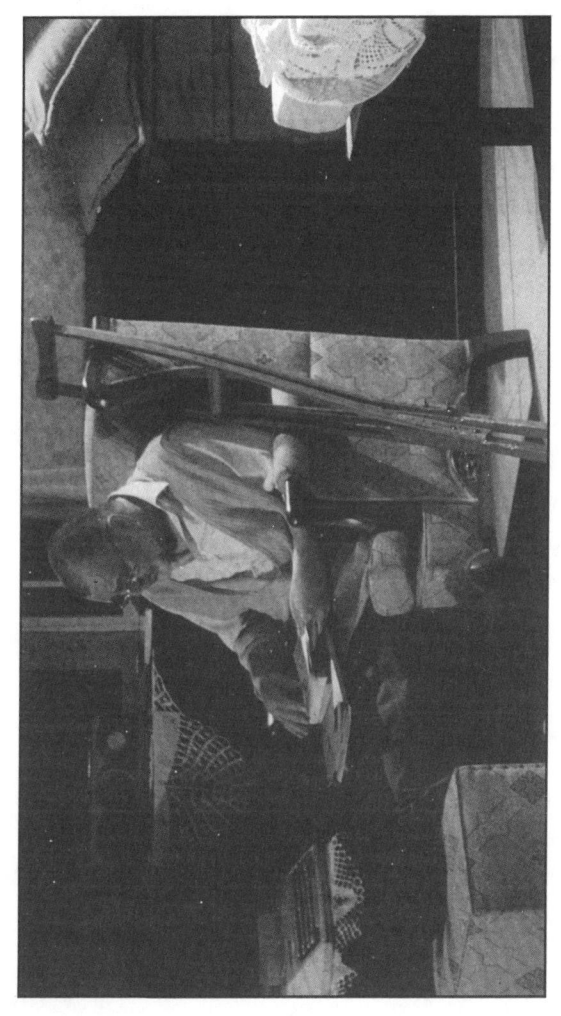

Mariano González as Segundo in world premiere of *El pasamanos (The Railing)*. Costa Rica, 1999. Directed by Marielos Fonseca.

THE RAILING

CHARACTERS

OSCAR FRESCO, a heavyset man in his 70s
ANGELA, his wife, in her 60s
MERCEDES CASTRO, TV journalist, mid 30s
RICARDO, TV cameraman, early 20s

(Translator's note: The original names of Oscar Fresco and Angela are Segundo Bueno and Adela. The changes, which have been made with Paloma Pedrero's permission, allow for comparable word games in English to those used by the author in the original text.)

SCENE ONE

As the lights come up, we see Oscar and Angela's apartment. It consists of a room with a small kitchen area along one wall. Although cramped, the place is cozy and carefully arranged. In the upstage wall we see a door to the bathroom. Downstage there is another door opening onto an old and steep hall stairway that leads down to a street door in an old neighborhood. OSCAR, a heavy-set old man in his seventies, is sitting in an easy chair. He's wearing a dark, out of style jacket and a white shirt. A pair of crutches lie beside his chair. ANGELA, his wife, is nervously moving about fussing with last minute preparations for a visit.

  It's mid-June, just beginning to get dark. A ray of late spring sunlight shines in through the one small window of the house.

ANGELA *(Handing OSCAR a frayed necktie)*: Take this, put it on. You should look like what you are. A gentleman.
OSCAR: Quit it now. Don't talk stupid, Angie. This tie's full of moth holes.
ANGELA: I'll tie it for you. I love to see you like that, dressed up and elegant.
OSCAR *(Throwing the tie aside)*: Help me put my new socks on. The navy blue ones.
ANGELA: It was your wedding tie. *(Smiling.)* When you opened the store you bought one just like it. You remember? One day you came home without it. You lost it. *(She keeps on fussing with the room.)*
OSCAR *(Raising his voice)*: Get me my new socks.
ANGELA *(Looking for them)*: You had new socks for the wedding, too. And shoes. Shoes with real leather soles. My sister told me how much she liked watching us kneeling at the altar, with your soles all nice and clean. . .
OSCAR: Put 'em on now.
ANGELA: Yes, sir. And then the tie you've had all our life. *(She starts putting on his socks.)*
OSCAR *(Whining)*: Be careful, Angie. Can't you see my feet are swollen?
ANGELA: Are you going to use your crutches?
OSCAR: Use them where?
ANGELA: Huh?
OSCAR *(Raising his voice)*: Use them where?
ANGELA: On the TV.
OSCAR: You better believe it. We'll see whether they believe I'm handicapped.
ANGELA: Huh?
OSCAR: Better believe they will.
ANGELA: Well then, give them to me. I'm going to clean them up.
OSCAR *(Looking at them)*: They *are* clean.
ANGELA: Give them to me.
OSCAR: Angie! They're clean as they can be!
ANGELA: I don't want anyone thinking we're messy.
OSCAR: Come on, Angie.
ANGELA *(Wiping the crutches, which OSCAR is holding, with a cloth)*: The TV catches everything. Even what it shouldn't. Sometimes people come on, and it's like they even seem to have bad breath.
OSCAR *(Looking in a hand mirror and fixing his hair)*: Get me my cologne. *(Raising his voice.)* My cologne.

ANGELA (*Holding up the bottle*): Should I put it on you?
OSCAR: Yes. (*ANGELA starts rubbing cologne on his feet.*) What are you doing?
ANGELA: Making you presentable. The TV doesn't miss a thing. Oscar, your feet smell bad.
OSCAR: Stop it! Stop fussing, Angie. My feet smell dead. Like they're dead. Understand? Not like cheese. Not alive. Everyday my circulation's worse. Shut up here like a prisoner; it's killing me little by little. First my feet. Then my legs, stiff. Then my parts, dead, everything. Everything in me wasting away because of those murderers.
ANGELA: Don't get all riled up now, Oscar. Save it to tell to the TV. Here, put your tie on and I'll fix the knot.
OSCAR (*Giving it a toss*): No! Can't you see it's old and faded?
ANGELA (*Picking up the tie*): You're just nervous. I don't like this TV business. (*Looks at the tie.*) There're no moth holes. (*Looks at the clock.*) They're going to be here any minute. You better go to the bathroom so you don't have to later.
OSCAR: Give me my brief. I need to look it over. (*ANGELA doesn't hear him.*) Give me the folder. Angie! Everything, those statutes, too, civil and criminal. Put them all right here, next to me. Bring that table over. (*ANGELA does so.*)
ANGELA: Do you have to take your pee?
OSCAR (*Looking over the stack of papers and books*): The whole country needs to know this stuff. All of it. I'm going to explain all of it. For one damn time I'm going to see some justice done.
ANGELA: Do you have to pee?
OSCAR: She won't be able to show her face. That *creature*. The whole country'll know Antonia Lopez Garcia is a murderer of the handicapped.
ANGELA: Take this.
OSCAR: What are you giving me?
ANGELA: Your ring.
OSCAR: What for?
ANGELA: Put it on, Oscar. It's gold. Your wedding ring. The TV catches everything. What will they think if they see you without your wedding ring?
OSCAR: You know it doesn't fit me. It cuts off my circulation.
ANGELA: It won't matter for a little bit. Then I'll get it off with soap.
OSCAR: My finger's dead. Swollen.
ANGELA: Here. I'll put it on.
OSCAR (*Raising his voice*): And if you can't get it off then?
ANGELA: We'll put olive oil on it. I'll rub it with olive oil, and it'll come right off.

(*OSCAR straightens out his ring finger with difficulty. ANGELA puts the ring on. She looks at him, pleased.*)

ANGELA: Now all you need is your tie.
OSCAR (*Looking at his hand. Nostalgic*): How many apples and cherries, and grapes and pears have these hands held? I used to love seeing the fruit, handling it. Just from touching it then I knew when it was good, when it was wormy. I only ever wanted my lady customers to be happy, so they'd come back again to Oscar Fresco's Market. "Fresh fruit. Worthy of an Oscar."

(*Lowering his voice.*) And they always used to laugh. How many good looking women have opened up their baskets to me...
ANGELA (*Even though she seems not to have been listening*): Yes. You always did like the ladies. They'd lean in with their shopping bag, and you'd put their fruit in, and take a good gander down their cleavage.
OSCAR: Angie...
ANGELA: I would see you, looking down there on the sly.
OSCAR: Have you put in your hearing aid?
ANGELA: Huh?
OSCAR (*Realizing the answer is no*): You hear what you want to hear, Angie. Your ear's sharp enough when you want, isn't it? A little of that's just in your head. More than a little, I'd say.
ANGELA: But I never worried because, like they say, barking dogs don't bite. (*Looking at him and smiling.*) I know you were always faithful. (*Fixing her hair.*)
OSCAR: You can't fool my guardian angel, Angie. She guesses everything.
ANGELA: Do I look all right? Am I presentable?
OSCAR: Put your hearing aid in. (*He makes a gesture of touching his ear.*)
ANGELA: Should I get the bedpan or do you want to go to the bathroom?
OSCAR (*Raising his voice*): Put your hearing aid in, Angie.
ANGELA (*Hesitating*): I... I'd rather not talk.
OSCAR: Well, put it in anyway. I want you to hear OK.
ANGELA: It's no difference. I hear bad either way. That hearing aid was a gyp.
OSCAR: You hear the same either way because you don't change the batteries. Give me the thing. Give it to me! And the batteries. (*She gives them to him reluctantly. He sets to fixing it.*) What a lot of fuss about not using it.
ANGELA: Everyone will see it.
OSCAR: Huh?
ANGELA: The TV catches everything. I don't like the idea of everyone in my hometown seeing me with some gadget sticking in my ear.
OSCAR: You're still a coquette.
ANGELA: What?
OSCAR: A vain little girl.
ANGELA: I don't like the thing. It doesn't work.
OSCAR (*Handing it to her*): Put it in. Let them put you on TV so they can see that I'm handicapped and you're deaf. That we're completely unprotected and defenseless. And give me the pension figures and the disability papers and the file with the medical expenses. (*Getting heated up.*) It's a shitty country. Shitty with the poor. Those two-bit politicians are all a joke. All alike. Getting fat, sucking on the power-tit.
ANGELA: Now don't get into that on TV. Don't get that into your head, Oscar.
OSCAR: Get into what?
ANGELA: The politicians. The administration and stuff. They'll get back at you. They run everything. You just concentrate on the railing for the stairs. Just the railing, you hear?
OSCAR: And justice. And loopholes in the law. I'm going to expose this whole rotten business–

ANGELA (*Interrupting him*): Go take your pee. (*She goes to him and helps him up. OSCAR, on his crutches, heads slowly towards the small bathroom. ANGELA opens the door for him.*) Do you need help?
OSCAR: I can manage. Thanks. Close the door.

(*We see MERCEDES coming up the stairs outside the apartment. She is a thirty-something, beauty-salon blonde, slightly affected in manner. Following her is an awkward young man with a camera on his shoulder.*)

MERCEDES: Really! This *is* a deathtrap. (*To the young man.*) Ricardo, get some shots of the entryway and the stairs. I'm going to go in up there. I'll let you know what's up in a minute.
RICARDO: Take your time. I'll have a smoke. (*After he takes a few shots, we see him roll a joint and sit down on the stairs to smoke it.*)
MERCEDES (*Knocks on the door. ANGELA opens it*): Good afternoon. I'm Mercedes Castro from the "Things of Life" show. (*ANGELA looks her up and down. Nods.*) Is this the apartment of Oscar Fresco?
ANGELA: Yes. Come in. Oscar's in the bathroom. I'm–
MERCEDES: You must be Angela, his wife. Right?
ANGELA: Yes. Angela del Castillo. Oscar's always called me Angie. (*She gestures as if waving a magic wand.*) His guardian angel, Angie. He says instead of walking I fly. Since I'm so tiny. . . but, sit down. What about the TV? The equipment for–
MERCEDES: Yes. The camera's coming in a minute. First I want to go over the interview with you. I need you to tell me a few things, confirm some information. (*Opens her briefcase.*) It's a fact that your husband hasn't left this place for nine years?
ANGELA: That's right. Miss Castro, would you like some coffee?
MERCEDES: No, thank you. I just had some. And how did this. . . ordeal get started? Tell me about it.
ANGELA: Wait. (*She knocks gently on the bathroom door.*) Oscar, Miss Castro is here. Do you need help?
OSCAR (*From inside*): I'm coming. I'll be there in a minute.
ANGELA (*To MERCEDES*): He takes a long time to do his business. But he doesn't like anybody to help him. You know, a typical man.
MERCEDES: Yes. I know.
ANGELA: It's easier in his pajamas. Today he got dressed, of course. Although he didn't want to put on his tie. (*Lowering her voice.*) Listen. My husband has a weak heart, you know. I didn't want him to do this television thing, but he's so stubborn.
MERCEDES: Don't worry, Angela. We only want to help him. His case impressed us a lot, and, well, we'd like to help him resolve this situation, this drama. I mean, I imagine it must be pretty hard on both of you. Isn't it?
ANGELA (*Watching the bathroom door*): What? (*Touching her ear.*) This thing only works when it feels like it.
MERCEDES (*Raising her voice*): I said I imagine it must be pretty hard on both of you, this situation. Isn't it?
ANGELA: Well, I'll tell you. We've gotten used to it. We manage. Oscar is reading up on it all the time. (*Indicates the books.*) He's learned a lot about the law.

When he was young, he wanted to be a lawyer. You know? It was his dream. But, of course, it was hard to go to school then without... (*Gestures "money" with her fingers.*) Now with this business of the lawsuit–

(*The bathroom door opens. OSCAR appears, walking very slowly on his crutches. MERCEDES gets up.*)

OSCAR: Good afternoon, Miss Castro. Excuse me, please.
MERCEDES: Please, relax, Oscar. There's no hurry. How are you?
OSCAR (*Offering his hand*): My pleasure. But sit down.
MERCEDES: How's it going? (*In a sympathetic tone.*) I imagine this situation could get you down.
OSCAR (*Sitting with ANGELA's help*): You can understand. Like a prison. Seeing life through that window. It's like I got a life sentence without committing a crime. My only crime is being crippled and poor.
MERCEDES: I'm here to help you, Oscar. My show has a big audience, and, although contributions aren't solicited, people often call in, and if the amount–
OSCAR (*Interrupting her. Angry*): I don't want charity, Miss Castro. I want justice.
MERCEDES: Yes, of course. Naturally. But the important thing, Oscar, is to resolve your problem, so you can get back outside again.
OSCAR: But to resolve it for the right reason. Not out of pity. Never.
MERCEDES (*Opening her briefcase*): Of course, of course. If you don't mind, I'd like to confirm some facts in my report on your case, and then we can get started. My cameraman is getting some shots of the stairway. Let's see. So, you're seventy, right?
OSCAR: Yes. Seventy in February.
MERCEDES: A fruit vendor by profession. A disability retirement at fifty-five. No children. (*OSCAR nods agreement.*) Nine years without being able to get outside because there's no stair railing to hold onto.
OSCAR: Exactly. One time I tried it, holding onto my wife. Imagine. Me weighing a hundred and ninety pounds and her only ninety. I fell down, of course. And only five steps to go. And I almost killed her. (*He looks at ANGELA.*) Because she's like a little angel, and if I–
ANGELA: And when they got him off of me, I couldn't breathe for a long time.
MERCEDES: That's awful! That's what you've got to tell us on camera.
OSCAR: And all because of eighty lousy bucks! You believe that?
MERCEDES: Terrible. And even more, sad and painful. Very painful.
OSCAR: After that fall, my left leg, which used to still bend a little, got stiff on me, like a broomstick. And look. (*He shows her his hand.*) I broke my ring finger. Since then it's been swollen and stiff.
ANGELA: He put his ring on today for the TV, but it would hardly fit.
MERCEDES: That's terrible, isn't it?
ANGELA: Well, we've gotten used to it–
OSCAR (*Almost talking over her*): It's humiliating! And it's all the fault of Antonia Lopez Garcia, the landlady of this place! And that bastard, her nephew! D'you know what they did one time? D' you know?
MERCEDES: Just a minute, Oscar. I'm going to get the cameraman, and we'll start filming. OK?

OSCAR: Get him in here. I'm ready to tell the whole works. I'll do in the lot of them.
MERCEDES (*Gets up and opens the door*): Ricardo! Ricardo, whenever you're ready.

(*RICARDO puts out his joint and comes up with his equipment.*)

RICARDO (*Coming in*): Afternoon.
OSCAR: Come in, young man. Good afternoon.
MERCEDES: Get everything ready and we'll start.
RICARDO: Where the old guy is, right?
MERCEDES: Right. The two of them, right there.

(*RICARDO sets his lights and hooks wireless mics to OSCAR and ANGELA.*)

RICARDO (*Putting the mic on OSCAR*): This is so they can hear you real good. OK, old buddy? (*Patting him on the shoulder.*)
OSCAR: Thanks, young fellow.
ANGELA: Miss Castro, wouldn't it be better if he put on his tie? Oscar has always been a smart dresser.
MERCEDES: Yes, of course. Whatever you two want.
OSCAR: Damn it, Angela. I'm not putting on the tie. And that's that.
ANGELA: Well, there're no moth holes in it.
OSCAR: But I don't like it.
ANGELA: Well then, that's another matter.
MERCEDES (*To ANGELA*): Now you sit right here, beside your husband.
ANGELA (*Situates herself as if for a photo*): Like this?
MERCEDES: That's right. Very good. It's important that you express whatever emotions you feel: indignation, suffering, pain. And if you feel like crying, you cry. Don't hesitate. Just cry. Our program wants to show raw reality, no holds barred. Always with the intention of helping, of course. So. Shall we start? Ready, Ricardo?
RICARDO: When you are, chief.
MERCEDES: Oscar. Are you ready?
OSCAR (*Unexpectedly*): But, Angela. You didn't offer these people coffee.
MERCEDES: Yes, she did. But we had some before we came up here. Thanks. Now. Ready?
OSCAR: OK. Ready.
ANGELA: Just a minute.
MERCEDES: Yes?
ANGELA: Does it matter if you don't show me from this side? I wouldn't like them to see my hearing aid. You know?
OSCAR: Angela! (*To Mercedes*) Don't pay any attention to her.
ANGELA: Well, I won't wear it, huh, Oscar?
RICARDO: Easy, Granny. I won't let it show.
ANGELA (*Covering it with her hair*): There.
MERCEDES: All ready now?

(*MERCEDES takes her place in front of them out of sight of the camera. From there she talks to them.*)

MERCEDES: Tell us, Oscar. Look at the camera and tell your unfortunate story.
OSCAR: We've lived here, in this building, for thirty years. In all that time I've never missed paying a single month of rent. Never. We've taken good care of it, like it was our own.
MERCEDES (*Interrupting him*): How many square feet is it?
OSCAR: It's 270 square feet. What you see here and the bathroom. I mean, for me, I would've liked to buy our own place, but, it wasn't possible. I worked as an employee in a fruit market until I was forty. At that age I went into debt up to my ears and started my own business. (*He gestures proudly with his hands.*) Oscar Fresco's Market. "Fresh fruit. Worthy of an Oscar." (*Smiling.*) That was my slogan. Five months after the business opened, they put up a huge supermarket right across the street. That was the end of my business.
MERCEDES: Tell me, Oscar, talk to the camera, when you started suffering with your legs, what happened with the railing?
OSCAR: We've never had a railing up to this floor, or, at least, not that I've known. But, you know, young and healthy, it wasn't so important. Fifteen years ago my legs started giving out.
MERCEDES: What's happening with your legs? How are they now?
OSCAR: Stiff and swollen. Almost dead.
MERCEDES: Do they hurt a lot?
OSCAR: Let's just say they hurt. But the worst thing is I can't get down to the street. (*He is getting angrier.*) I can't go downstairs without holding onto something. It's impossible. I mean, since my fall–
MERCEDES: Tell us about your fall. (*She signals the camera to cut for a moment.*) Oscar, everything's going fine, but I'd like you to put a little more. . . how can I say it. . . bring out more of your suffering and show it. You understand me?
OSCAR: Suffering? Well imagine, just imagine what it's like to live like this. Not being able to breathe fresh air, not seeing the kids out playing, not being able to sit in the park and take in the sun, not being able to throw crumbs to the pigeons. I mean, I put some out for them on the window sill, and they come and eat it, right, but it's not the same. (*He looks at ANGELA and gets more emotional.*) And my wife, always alone on the street, without a husband, or worse yet, with a hundred and ninety pound burden waiting at home for her. (*ANGELA shakes her head denying this.*) And also, it's very dangerous for her to be going up and down like that, without protection, with her grocery money in her shopping bag. And all because of a lack of humanity. All because the landlady of this property, Antonia Lopez Garcia, wants us out of here!
MERCEDES: Has she said that to you?
OSCAR: Yes. Indirectly. She'd like us to go off to some old people's home so she can sell this place and make a bundle. Can you believe that? After thirty years she wants to send us off to rot away in some institution. So. That's the truth of it. She want us to get out of here. And if not that, for me to die. Kill me from suffering; that's what she's trying to do. (*Angry.*) But she's not going to get her way, because I'm going to win this case. Look at what I've got here: papers and more papers. I win the case, she appeals, and back to the

beginning. Years of that. She refuses to spend the eighty dollars the railing costs, and, of course, for so little money, no one will lift a finger... (*Looking hard at the camera.*) Antonia Lopez Garcia, I'll see them bury you. Me, Oscar Fresco Anton. I'll walk down those stairs holding onto a railing that you're going to put there for me before you die.

MERCEDES (*Interrupts him, trying to change the subject*): Oscar, tell us. What do you feel in a situation like this? Tell us from the heart.

OSCAR: Impotence, Miss. Impotence. I won a judgment two years ago, and they ordered her to put up a handrail for me. You know what she did? She sent her degenerate nephew over here with a rope. Really. He ran some string from the top to the bottom of the stairs, not even tied in right. Three sticks and a rope, and she had done us a big favor.

MERCEDES: And what did you do?

OSCAR: Me, I sent the rope back to her with a note.

MERCEDES: Really? Which said?

OSCAR: Go hang yourself with this.

MERCEDES: Cut, Ricardo.

OSCAR: What's the matter?

ANGELA: That doesn't make you look good, Oscar. Don't you see that?

OSCAR: I have to tell the truth. I did it, and I admit it.

MERCEDES: It's OK. Don't worry. We'll edit it later for the show. That's right, we keep the most important stuff and, of course, all the stuff that can help. Listen, it would be interesting if you would talk to us a little more about the pain; you did that really well before. For example, talk to us about what you do during an interminable day of being shut up in here. Also, it would be interesting for you to show your bad legs on camera.

OSCAR: Not a chance! I'm crippled, and I'm poor, but I have my pride.

ANGELA: You can understand, Miss Castro. It's just that my husband doesn't like things like that.

OSCAR: What I want to do is speak out against a situation of social injustice. To show that the law is even more rotten than my old legs, that it always favors the guys with the money.

ANGELA: Not that, Oscar. Don't start talking about politics.

MERCEDES (*Drily*): But what you want is for them to put up a railing for you. Right?

OSCAR: Yes, Miss Castro. And that it's put up by the person who's supposed to put it up.

MERCEDES (*A little fed up with him*): So then, I think with our lead-in to the case, some part of what we've shot, the footage of the stairs... I don't know. I think there's something of the emotional stuff missing. The pain is the thing that always gets the audience worked up, but I can see that you–

OSCAR: I'm still a man, Miss Castro, and my brain still works.

ANGELA: And other things, too... (*RICARDO laughs.*)

MERCEDES (*Slightly flustered*): Well good. I don't doubt that, but, we've got to get people stirred up. To stir them up means–

ANGELA (*Interrupting her*): If you like, it's easier for me to cry. If you think we can't do without it.

MERCEDES: OK. Not a bad idea. It can help us round out the story. Let's go for it.

ANGELA (*To the cameraman, indicating her hearing aid*): Can you see it?
RICARDO: No, Granny, don't you worry.
ANGELA (*Concentrating*): Say when.
MERCEDES (*Giving RICARDO a signal*): Tell me, Angela. Tell us how you stand living in this hell. What's it like?
ANGELA (*Tearful*): Bad. It's terrible seeing my husband shut in for so many years. Someone who always liked being out on the street so much. Nobody knows what we're going through. (*Covering her face with her hands.*)
MERCEDES: Very good, Angela. Thank you. Would it be all right if we took a few shots of some daily activity? It could be. . . Oscar going over to the bathroom sink, or looking sadly out the window. Another one with Angela helping him to neaten himself up.
OSCAR: If that's the only way to do it.
MERCEDES: The truth is, quite honestly, to get to the audience's heart and to the justice of the thing, I think it would be very important for you to show us the condition of your legs, I mean, carefully, with dignity.
OSCAR: No, ma'am. My legs are puffed up and stiff. They're not very nice to look at.
MERCEDES: Oscar, think about your objective. Think about the hit she's going to take. (*Looking at her file.*) This Antonia Lopez.
OSCAR: That woman doesn't suffer or feel anything.
MERCEDES: Oscar, I need your cooperation. I mean, sitting there like that nobody gets any idea of the seriousness of your physical problem. We have to make an impression on public opinion. Don't you realize that? You, all you have to do is pull up your pants legs a little. For example, while Angela is helping you put on your shoes. What do you think?
OSCAR (*Showing her his papers again*): Look, here are nine years of my life. My lawyer sits here beside me, and between us we figure out how to–
MERCEDES (*Cutting him off*): I'm sorry, Oscar, but we have to wrap up here.
OSCAR: But you haven't let me explain the details of–
MERCEDES: Don't worry now. My team and I, when we work up the story for the show, we'll explain all that. I've got those facts in my briefcase here. You understand? OK. Can we get these shots? I don't have much time.
ANGELA: Oscar, Miss Castro is getting annoyed.
OSCAR: And she's always so sweet on the TV.
MERCEDES: I need you to cooperate with me. We're doing this for you, and I know what works on television. Don't you realize that? With what we've got and these shots we can put together a hard-hitting story. Trust me.

(*OSCAR and ANGELA look at each other. OSCAR shrugs his shoulders. ANGELA stands up and then gets down on her knees at OSCAR's feet.*)

MERCEDES: Thank you. One minute. Take their mics off, Ricardo. They don't need them now. (*RICARDO does so.*) Let's shoot it.
ANGELA (*Starts to take off her husband's shoes*): The TV catches everything, just like I told you.
OSCAR (*Disgusted*): Don't pull them up too high.
ANGELA: What?
OSCAR: The pants.

ANGELA: I still like your legs, Oscar. I like them because I knew them when they were strong and healthy.
OSCAR: And now they're dead.
ANGELA: Not dead, no. They still hold you up OK. Just deaf like my ears. (*She smiles. The camera is over OSCAR's legs.*) Show your ring. Come on, Oscar, show it for the TV. You didn't tell them we've been married almost fifty years.
OSCAR (*Sweetly, placing his hand on her head in order to show the ring to the camera*): Oh, Angie, Angie. . .

(*The lights go to black.*)

SCENE TWO

Three days later. As the lights come up, we see the staircase sporting a recently installed railing. Inside the apartment ANGELA is preparing breakfast. OSCAR is lying on the bed.

ANGELA: Come on, Oscar. The coffee's ready.
OSCAR: Bring it over here.
ANGELA: Not on your life. You're going to get up right this minute, and you're going to eat breakfast with me at the table, the same as always.
OSCAR: I don't feel like it.
ANGELA: You have to stop bothering your head about this and cheer up. Forget it, now. Forget it.
OSCAR: How can I forget it? They deceived me. They deceived us, Angie. They didn't include my accusation. They said things that I didn't say. They went to the landlady's, and that disgusting woman called me a fraud. She said that I lied, that I'm not as sick as I say I am, that I only live to squabble with her and to win my case.
ANGELA: Don't get in such an uproar, Oscar. Calm down.
OSCAR: Why didn't that reporter woman tell us she was going to talk with her? I would have pointed out a few things. I would have filled her in on what that woman is like.
ANGELA: Forget it, now. Don't keep torturing yourself. It's not worth the agony.
OSCAR: And those horrible pictures of my legs. Close-ups of swollen bruises.
ANGELA: OK. It's over. You can't keep going around and around about it. We did it and it's done. So now it's over. We forget about it and go back to our normal, quiet life, without the commotion.
OSCAR: That Miss Castro didn't let me explain myself. She didn't let me tell her about the last suit I filed.
ANGELA: They do things in their own way. I told you so. I warned you about the TV tricks. But you were so sure of yourself.
OSCAR: She always seemed so nice on the TV.
ANGELA: Don't worry yourself about it anymore. It's not all that important. I mean, it's not important at all.
OSCAR: You don't think so?
ANGELA: How's it going to be important? Say what you like, that woman is not nice and doesn't have a case; that ended up being clear.
OSCAR: You think so?
ANGELA: Lordy, Oscar. It's almost better they did show her. Let everybody see her old witch face, a messy old woman, warts and all. Those disgraceful eyes.
OSCAR: Yes. She has that look with no soul behind it.
ANGELA: And now, what you have to do is think about continuing your case. That's your strength, Oscar. Your books, your papers. (*She looks at him admiringly.*) I mean, you already know as much as a lawyer.
OSCAR (*Pulling himself together*): You're right. I have to continue down the legal path. Give me my crutches. I'm going to get up.
ANGELA: That's how I like to hear you talk. (*She gives them to him and helps him get up.*)
OSCAR: And did you notice, Angie, how it was with the batteries?

ANGELA: The what?
OSCAR: Don't you notice how well you hear now with your hearing aid?
ANGELA: Ah, the gadget. I mean, it depends on how the day's going.
OSCAR: Now don't be silly.
ANGELA: Come on. Drink your coffee. (*OSCAR, helped by ANGELA, sits at the table.*)
OSCAR: And you couldn't see it on the TV.
ANGELA: What?
OSCAR: The hearing aid. You couldn't see it.
ANGELA: Let's forget the whole business, Oscar. You've been obsessed with it for three days.
OSCAR: I hadn't told you that.
ANGELA: And you didn't need to.
OSCAR: OK, but since you were so worried about it. . . But no, you looked very pretty.
ANGELA: Pretty? How can you say that? On there, all crying. I thought they'd put a little make-up on me, some powder. I'm sure they do up Miss Castro's face for the show. How she changed, didn't she? Because the day she came here, she was pretty ugly.
OSCAR: And she didn't let me explain to her–
ANGELA: Sh! Shush. It's over. Now then. Finish breakfast so you can get back to work. I'm going to go grocery shopping. And I'm going to buy a couple of nice steaks to celebrate everything getting back to just like before. Happy day! Shall I bring over your books? Your briefcase?
OSCAR (*Determined*): Yes. Give me all the papers. I'm going to work through the appeal all over again.
ANGELA (*Happy, she cleans the table and brings him the papers*): Do you need anything from the drugstore?
OSCAR: Yes, my heart medicine's almost gone.
ANGELA: Then I'll go by the doctor's for the prescription. (*She gets her shopping bag and jacket.*) Anything else? (*He shakes his head no.*) I'll be right back.

(*ANGELA opens the apartment door and sees the stair railing in place. She lets out a smothered shriek.*)

ANGELA: Oh my God! Oh my God!
OSCAR (*From inside*): What's the matter? What's the matter, Angie?
ANGELA (*She enters, upset*): Oscar. They put it up. They put it up.
OSCAR: They put what up?
ANGELA: The railing.
OSCAR: How? What do you mean?
ANGELA (*Nodding her head*): The railing. They've put it up.
OSCAR: But. . . how? When? Who put it up?
ANGELA: How do I know? I didn't hear anything. I mean, did you?
OSCAR (*Thinking*): Maybe last night. Yeah, last night, while we were listening to the radio, I heard some noise. A few. . . I thought it was the rats. Come on, help me, Angie. Help me up. I want to see it.

(*Trembling, the two of them approach the landing at the top of the stairs.*)

ANGELA: Look.
OSCAR (*He lets out a low cry*): Yes. It's true.
ANGELA (*She slowly touches it as if to assure herself that it's not a dream.*) Oh, it's. . . It's fastened. It doesn't move.
OSCAR: You sure?
ANGELA (*Checking the hardware.*) They've screwed it into the woodwork.
OSCAR: Looks like pine. A pine railing.
ANGELA (*Rubbing her hand over it.*) Varnished.
OSCAR: Give it a good tug. Be sure it's hooked in tight. It could be a trap.
ANGELA (*Trying to move it*): Yes. It's real tight. Look. Nobody's going to move that.
OSCAR (*Suddenly*): She's given up! Finally! Antonia Lopez Garcia has given up. We did it, Angie. Now that people have seen that witch on the TV, she must be dying of shame. You were right, Angie. Someone put the pressure on her. Her lawyer must have told her she was done for.
ANGELA: But why did they do it like this? Why didn't they tell us?
OSCAR (*Still thinking hard.*) I don't know. Come on. Let's go inside. We have to think about this.

(*They go into the apartment and close the door.*)

(*We see MERCEDES CASTRO appear at the bottom of the staircase. She comes in with the cameraman, RICARDO. He starts lighting the stairs. MERCEDES slowly goes up the stairs and knocks on the apartment door. Then she comes down the stairs and speaks to the cameraman.*)

MERCEDES: Action!
ANGELA: Who could that be?
OSCAR: Ask.
ANGELA: Who is it? Who is it? (*To OSCAR.*) There's no answer.
OSCAR: Don't open it.
ANGELA (*Scared.*) Do you think it's. . .
OSCAR: I don't trust her. Maybe it's. . . She may be furious and want to hurt us. Don't open it.
ANGELA: What do we do?
OSCAR: Look through the peephole.
ANGELA (*She does. A startled reaction*): There's light. Lots of light. A terrible light.
OSCAR (*Frightened. Shouting*): Who's there? What do you want from us?

(*MERCEDES, seeing that they are not opening the door, creeps up the stairs and knocks on the door. Then she goes back down toward the camera.*)

MERCEDES (*To RICARDO*): Be ready. You have to catch the moment. Their faces, their look when they see the railing.
RICARDO: Got you, chief.
MERCEDES: And put out that joint. Jesus!
RICARDO (*Tossing it away, unwillingly*): You got it, yo!

OSCAR: Look again.
ANGELA: There's no one, Oscar. There's no one.
OSCAR (*Terrified*): She's getting us back. Wants to scare us.
ANGELA: We better open it.
OSCAR: Don't you dare. She might have sent somebody. . . with a knife.
ANGELA: What for?
OSCAR: They're forcing open the door.
ANGELA: I don't hear anything. I don't hear anything. (*Terrified, she pulls her hearing aid out and throws it on the floor.*)
MERCEDES (*To RICARDO*): They're probably still asleep. I'm going to keep trying. You be ready. (*Goes up and knocks again.*)
OSCAR (*Shouting*): I'm calling the police right now. You hear me? Whoever you are? You hear? I'm calling the police.
MERCEDES (*Hearing him. Surprised. She comes up to the door*): Oscar. It's me. Calm down. It's the TV people.
OSCAR: Who are you?
MERCEDES: Mercedes Castro. Open the door. Please. And calm down. We've got a surprise for you.
OSCAR (*Perplexed. Looking at ANGELA*): It's Miss Castro.
ANGELA: What?
OSCAR: Miss Castro. From the television.
ANGELA: What does she want?
MERCEDES (*From outside*): Open the door, Oscar. And come out on the landing.

(*MERCEDES steps back so as not to block the camera.*)

ANGELA: What does she want?
OSCAR: She says she has a surprise. (*The two look at each other, catching on at the same time.*) The railing! They're the ones who put it up. (*OSCAR opens the door and slowly but deliberately walks to the top of the stairs.*)
MERCEDES (*From down below, overblown*): Oscar, the program "Things of Life" takes great satisfaction in seeing your wish become a reality. And we want to be with you at this crucial moment of your life, when, finally, after nine years of captivity, you will once again walk down the stairs and out to the street–
OSCAR (*Rudely interrupting her*): Who put up the stair railing?
MERCEDES: We wanted to surprise you and be with you–
OSCAR: Who put the thing up?
MERCEDES: Our tech crew. We didn't let you know because we wanted to see it, to live this moment with you–
OSCAR: Who put it up?
MERCEDES (*Getting nervous*): Last night. I think it was pretty simple. It was just a question of screwing it to the woodwork. You see, Oscar, how simple the solution to your problem was–
OSCAR (*Aggressively*): Who paid for it?
MERCEDES: You see, after the program, viewers started calling in, volunteering donations and–

(*OSCAR raises his crutch and starts beating furiously on the stair rail.*)

OSCAR: Get out of here! Get out! Get this thing out of here! Get this offensive thing out of here! I asked for justice! Justice!
MERCEDES *(To RICARDO)*: Cut! Cut!
ANGELA *(Trying to hold OSCAR back)*: Oscar, calm down. Please. You know, you're going to make yourself sick.
OSCAR: Justice. Not pity. No pity! No pity! *(He gets quiet, out of breath.)*
ANGELA: Just calm down. Calm down. Please. *(She touches him gently.)* It's all right. It's all right.

(MERCEDES, touched by this, comes up the stairs and approaches OSCAR.)

MERCEDES: I'm sorry. I thought you needed a railing for the stairs. I thought the important thing was to solve your problem.
ANGELA: Let's go inside. I'm going to make some tea.
MERCEDES *(To RICARDO, indicating his cellular phone)*: I'll let you know when I need you.
RICARDO *(With a gesture)*: OK. I'll be in the bar downstairs having a beer. *(He starts collecting his stuff.)*

(The three go into the apartment. ANGELA helps OSCAR sit down in his easy chair.)

MERCEDES: How are we doing?
OSCAR: Bad. How would you like me to be? You played a fast one on me.
MERCEDES: Don't say that. It's not true. I only tried to help you.
OSCAR: Help me? How?
MERCEDES: The story about your case was a smash, a real social shocker. Our show plays to a huge audience, you know that. The viewers called in by the thousands offering their support. Everybody wanted to join in and help you out of your tragic situation.
OSCAR: You put the landlady on the show.
MERCEDES: We have to do it that way. You have to air the opinions of both parties in the conflict. It wouldn't be fair if we didn't do that.
OSCAR: But you didn't tell me that. I would have explained some things.
MERCEDES: I know what the woman's like. She's tight-fisted and ignorant.
OSCAR: No. Ignorant. Not a bit. That woman knows very well what she's doing.
MERCEDES: The upshot of her appearing on the show turned out favorable for you. Everybody commented on how outrageous the landlady's position was, how wrong she was.
OSCAR: I want them to take down the railing. Right now.
MERCEDES: Come on, now! How can you say that?
OSCAR: Either Antonia Lopez Garcia pays for the railing or these hands *(holding them up)* never touch it. I mean it, Miss Castro. They'll never touch it.
ANGELA: Have your tea, Oscar. Would you like some, Miss Castro?
MERCEDES: No, thank you.
ANGELA: When are you going to take down the railing?
MERCEDES *(Upset)*: Oh, Angela. You, too? Don't you realize your husband needs it?
ANGELA: You scared us to death.

MERCEDES: I'm sorry. I didn't think it would scare you like that. All we wanted was to give you a nice surprise.

ANGELA: We don't want to be on the TV again. It was a mistake. The TV picks up everything; even the stuff it shouldn't. Take the railing away and forget about us.

MERCEDES: I don't understand you two. Really. You asked for help from the show because you needed a stair railing.

OSCAR: We needed to report a miscarriage of justice. I told you that. I don't want pity. Look here. I've been nine years without going outside, studying law to act in my case, fighting for a cause. You can't come in here now with your camera and your money and ruin the whole thing.

MERCEDES: I don't know what to say to you.

OSCAR: Call and tell your crew to take the thing away.

MERCEDES (*Lashing back*): Can't you see you're not making sense?

OSCAR: No, I can't.

MERCEDES: You don't want to solve your problem. What you want is to take revenge on someone. That's not a very ethical attitude.

OSCAR: I've already explained my reasons. It seems to me you just don't want to hear me.

MERCEDES: I think I'm beginning to understand.

OSCAR: Then listen, please. Just leave things the way they were a week ago.

MERCEDES: I can't. I have to close tomorrow's show with a wrap up for this story.

OSCAR: I'm not a story. I'm a human being.

MERCEDES (*Trying to put on a cordial tone*): Listen. I want to help you. I really do. But I think you're being pig-headed. Why don't you forget your old grudges and think about the plaza with the pigeons and the kids playing and the springtime?

OSCAR (*Grabbing his papers*): I assure you I'm going to get all of that soon enough.

MERCEDES: I have a suggestion. What you want is for the landlady to pay for the railing. Is that right?

OSCAR: That's right.

MERCEDES: I suggest we finish the story. You get dressed, look your handsome best, your wife, too. And the two of you come out together smiling into the street. And I promise you, afterwards, I'll go to see the landlady and make sure she pays the bill for the railing. And I promise also to bring the check back with her signature on it. What do you think?

OSCAR: I don't trust that woman.

MERCEDES: Then trust me.

OSCAR: I don't trust you either.

ANGELA: When are they going to take down the railing?

MERCEDES (*Ignoring ANGELA*): I assure you I have ways of getting that woman to—

OSCAR: Listen, Miss Castro. Why don't you get on another case? There are a lot of problems in this country. In this city. In this neighborhood. Why are you so set on solving mine?

MERCEDES: Because you asked me to. And besides, I'm a professional. When I start a job, I have to finish it.

OSCAR: I don't understand you.
MERCEDES: I have to wrap up this story for tomorrow's show. But besides that, and most of all, your case interests the viewers. The happy ending's been announced. That's the way I thought it was going to happen. That's the way I set it up to happen. I can't disappoint my director or my public.
OSCAR: The happy ending's been announced?
MERCEDES: Yes. Didn't you two see the preview of the show?
OSCAR (*Perplexed, shaking his head*): What do you want me to do?
MERCEDES: I'd like to shoot the moment when you step out on the street after nine years. Your descent down the stairs holding onto the railing.
OSCAR: Not that. I'm not going to touch it until it's put up by the person with the obligation to do it. I've decided to follow a legal path.
ANGELA: Leave him in peace. Can't you see it's his life?
MERCEDES: From what I can see you don't want to go out to the street. You don't care beans about the railing.
OSCAR (*Angry*): Look lady. I can't give up my rights. Not now. That handrail is a right. I don't want your charity.
MERCEDES (*After a pause*): All right. I'll make do with what's happened. I'll finish the story with another ending. . . that's not so happy.
OSCAR: What's that supposed to mean?
MERCEDES: I'll tell the truth: that you really didn't want the railing.
OSCAR: That's a lie.
MERCEDES: OK. I have you on tape, Oscar, beating on the handrail with your crutch. Clearly you don't want it. So anyway, it's not a bad solution. Of course, I'm sorry for you. I would have liked so much seeing you in the street, seeing you happy.
OSCAR: You can't show those pictures.
MERCEDES: Why not? They're real. Of you. I didn't take them in your apartment.
OSCAR: They could damage me. Don't you understand? I'm in the middle of a lengthy legal action. An action that could be decided in a few months. An action that I'm going to win. If you show those pictures on television–
MERCEDES: They shouldn't carry any weight. You can explain why you did it.
OSCAR (*Visibly nervous*): But they could work against me. The landlady could use them.
ANGELA (*To MERCEDES*): So then, when are you going to take down the railing?
OSCAR: Put in your hearing aid, Angie! (*Begging her with a look.*) Put it in! (*ANGELA does so and looks at MERCEDES.*)
MERCEDES: Now then. We were talking about the railing.
ANGELA: You scared us to death.
MERCEDES: I'm sorry. But I don't understand why you're so afraid.
ANGELA: That woman's threatened us before. She's tried to scare us a number of times. She's got it in for us.
OSCAR (*Extremely upset. To MERCEDES*): You can't show those pictures. They could cause me to lose the case.
MERCEDES: You decide.
OSCAR: Me decide? You won't let me decide. None of your options is acceptable. Please, I'm asking you. Leave things the way they were. Take down the railing and let's forget it–

MERCEDES: (*Interrupting him firmly*): And what do I tell my viewers? How do I explain spending the money they sent in?
OSCAR (*Stymied*): I don't know.
MERCEDES: If I just leave your case up in the air, people will get suspicious.
OSCAR: Suspicious?
MERCEDES: Of course. And I can't take that chance with my job. Life's tough for everybody, right?
OSCAR (*Cornered*): I don't know. I don't understand why everything's gotten so complicated. I don't know.
ANGELA: What's the matter?
OSCAR (*Desperate*): She wants to show me on the TV beating on the railing.
MERCEDES: That's not what I want, Oscar. You're forcing me to do it.
ANGELA: Miss Castro. Listen to me. You're young. You're healthy. You have everything in life. The world's full of horrible stuff you can catch with your TV. We. . . my husband. . . is fighting for just one cause. One single cause. Do you understand? You have to let him do that.
MERCEDES: Tell me, Oscar. Tell me exactly what you want.
OSCAR: She, the landlady of this apartment, is the one who has to put up the railing. By law.
MERCEDES: All right. Let's come to an agreement. I'm going to see to it that Antonia Lopez is the one to pay for the handrail. What's more, you will write the document you want, and I, I will go talk to her and bring it back to you, signed.
OSCAR: You won't be able to.
MERCEDES: Oh yes I will. I know that woman. I interviewed her. She lives in the neighborhood.
OSCAR: Unfortunately.
MERCEDES: I'll see to it she fulfills her obligation. Your landlady will guarantee me full payment for the railing. Signed, sealed, and delivered. What do you say?
OSCAR (*Shrugging his shoulders*): I don't think she'll agree.
MERCEDES (*With renewed energy*): You write the document, yourself.
OSCAR (*Beaten down and confused*): The document?
MERCEDES: Yes. Write down on a piece of paper what you want the landlady to sign.
OSCAR: Wait. Let me think. (*Without recourse.*) Angie, bring me the typewriter. (*She does. He puts in a sheet of paper and thinks. He writes something, has a doubt, pulls out the paper, and tears it up. He puts in another and starts writing. He finishes, pulls out the paper and leaves it on the table. Intimidated, he says:*) I have to go to the bathroom.
ANGELA (*Helping him up*): Are you all right?
MERCEDES: Have you finished the document, Oscar?
OSCAR: Yes. I think so. (*With difficulty he heads towards the bathroom.*)
MERCEDES (*Reading aloud*): I, Antonia Lopez Garcia, proprietress of the apartment inhabited by Oscar Fresco Anton, in his capacity as leaseholder, and located at number four, Laurel Street, hereby agree to pay for the stair railing at said property, recognizing myself as the party with whom such obligation for payment corresponds and for installation of the same. Signed by me on this day. . . OK. It seems very much in order.

OSCAR: I'm sorry. I have to get by.
MERCEDES: I'm going to bring you this signature, Oscar. (*OSCAR goes into the bathroom. ANGELA helps him close the door.*) Now, Angela, I'm going to take care of this little piece of business. Meantime, you two get yourselves ready–
ANGELA: You've hurt him.
MERCEDES: Everything is going to work out. You'll see.
ANGELA: You're a thoughtless person.
MERCEDES: Listen to me a minute. The handrail's installed, and, finally, you two are going to begin a new life. I think your husband is a little bit in shock over it. It makes sense, so many years stuck here. But you could help him–
ANGELA: I don't need your advice, Miss Castro, thank you. How are you going to get her signature?
MERCEDES: That's my business.
ANGELA: He knows that woman's signature like his own. Don't try to fool him, because–
MERCEDES: She'll sign it. I give you my word.
ANGELA: God help us.
MERCEDES (*Putting the letter in her pocketbook*): I'm going now. (*Looks at her watch.*) I didn't think there would be so many complications. You get ready. I'll be back soon.

(*ANGELA opens the door for her. MERCEDES leaves. ANGELA waits until she's gone, then goes out to look at the railing. She moves over to it, turns around, thinking. Suddenly she decides something and goes back into the apartment.*)

ANGELA (*Muttering*): Oscar. Oscar. He's the only one who matters. (*Knocks on the bathroom door.*) Oscar. She's gone now. Oscar. You hear me? (*Frightened.*) Oscar? (*The door opens slowly. OSCAR appears and looks around. ANGELA smiles and speaks firmly.*) Oscar. Look at me. Today. You and me. We're going to go out together and take in the spring.

(*The lights go to black.*)

Anabelle de Garrido (Adela) attempts to revive Mariano González (Segundo). *El pasamanos* (*The Railing*), Costa Rica, 1999. Directed by Marielos Fonseca.

FINAL SCENE

Around noon of the same day. Dressed to the hilt, OSCAR and ANGELA are playing cards.

ANGELA: Draw. Come on, it's your draw. (*He draws one.*) Discard. (*He does so in an automatic way.*) Poor baby. Some luck with the trump.
OSCAR (*Throwing down the cards*): Let's forget this, Angie.
ANGELA (*Animated*): What do you think about trying it out? So, probably now we can't go down even with the railing. (*Laughing.*) Imagine that! Probably now we need two railings. So, what a fuss!
OSCAR: She's not coming back. That woman's not going to pay.
ANGELA: I bet she will. That Miss Castro knows what she's doing.
OSCAR: It's getting late.
ANGELA: Don't get impatient. Come on. Let's give it a little try?
OSCAR: Angela!
ANGELA: We've got stuck thinking only about ourselves. Haven't we? To heck with the rest of the world! To heck with them! Let's fix our life up again, Oscar. Today, right now, let's go down to the corner and have a nice *café con leche*.
OSCAR: She has to bring back the check: the signed check.
ANGELA: Are you going to put your ring on? The other day it came off easy with the soap. Shall I get it for you?
OSCAR: Give me the files.
ANGELA: The files? What for? Come on, Oscar. You promised to forget this now. You promised only to think about us now. About you, and about. . . me. (*She takes his hand.*) I'm going to walk down beside you, the two of us together. As if it were our wedding day stairs. Give me your finger. (*He does. She puts the ring on.*)
OSCAR: Angie. . .
ANGELA: What?
OSCAR: You were right. It was a mistake. I made a mistake calling the TV. Are young people all like this? Is this what all the young people are like?
ANGELA: Like what?
OSCAR: Like Miss Castro. It's been so long since I've talked to a young person. I only know what the world's like from the TV. And the TV's full of rotten lies.
ANGELA: Do you want a little tea? Some camomile tea with a little brandy?
OSCAR: And what if she doesn't pay for it?
ANGELA: She'll pay for it. Don't worry. She'll pay for it. You know what I'm thinking? This afternoon we'll walk down all the way to the new fruit stand. The owner's such a nice young man. Listen, you could even offer to lend him a hand. You could handle the register.
OSCAR: You look very pretty. (*She smiles, pleased.*)

(*MERCEDES comes in with RICARDO.*)

MERCEDES: Get ready now. Quick.
RICARDO: Crazy day. Hey, partner?
MERCEDES (*She goes up the stairs and knocks on the door.*) It's me. (*ANGELA opens. MERCEDES rushes in like a whirlwind.*) Good news. (*She hands the paper to OSCAR.*) Here it is.

MERCEDES (*She goes up the stairs and knocks on the door.*) It's me. (*ANGELA opens. MERCEDES rushes in like a whirlwind.*) Good news. (*She hands the paper to OSCAR.*) Here it is.
OSCAR (*Looks at it thoroughly)*: Yes. That's her signature. How did you do it?
MERCEDES: The woman didn't have a leg to stand on. No way.
OSCAR: But you took so long.
MERCEDES: No longer than necessary. Your landlady surrendered to my arguments, Oscar.
OSCAR: Your arguments?
MERCEDES: And yours, of course.
OSCAR: And how did she pay for it?
MERCEDES: Well, OK. Evidently she didn't have the cash. But, she's going to make a transfer right away this morning to our account.
OSCAR (*Starts shaking his head, negating this idea)*: That's not what we agreed to. That is not–
MERCEDES (*Interrupting him, sharply)*: I'm not arguing with you about it. I'm telling you the truth, and you have to believe me. Oscar, I can't devote all the hours of my life just to you.
ANGELA (*With the document in hand)*: She's given up for sure now. Thrown in the towel. This is really your victory. Don't you see that? (*OSCAR looks at his wife, defeated, without the strength to speak.*)
MERCEDES: Are you ready to shoot?
ANGELA: Yes.
MERCEDES (*To OSCAR)*: Congratulations.

(*MERCEDES opens the door and goes out. The stairs are already lighted. OSCAR, shaking and silent, can't make up his mind.*)

ANGELA: Come on, Oscar. You look very elegant. Only your tie is missing.
OSCAR (*Bending his head down)*: Put it on. (*She does.*)

(*OSCAR goes over to the edge of the stairs and looks at the railing.*)

ANGELA: You want me to help you?
OSCAR: No. I have to do it by myself. You at my side.

(*OSCAR doesn't seem to dare touch the railing. Then suddenly he lets out a sigh and lets go of one crutch, and with that hand he firmly grabs hold of the railing.*)

MERCEDES (*From the bottom of the stairs)*: You need help?
OSCAR: No.

(*OSCAR seems not to be able to take a step down. There is a tense silence, everybody watching him. He tries to grab hold a different way. His arms are shaking. His enormous effort shows in his face. Finally he manages to go down one step.*)

OSCAR (*To MERCEDES)*: There now. You can start filming whenever you want.

The Railing - 53

MERCEDES (*Gives the cue to RICARDO*): Thanks, Oscar. I want you to know that, in spite of all the problems, or, maybe, because of them, I'm very moved. I'm moved and happy to be able to witness your first steps out to the street.

(*OSCAR, without listening to her, continues slowly down the stairs. At his side, like a guardian angel, is ANGELA. When they're just four steps from the bottom, he raises his head, breathing hard. He looks at ANGELA, his eyes strange.*)

ANGELA: Oscar. Are you all right?
OSCAR: They tricked us, Angie.

(*OSCAR suddenly lets go of the other crutch and grabs the railing with both hands. He starts slipping and falls gently to the steps. ANGELA tries to hold him up but, lacking the strength, falls lightly on top of him.*)

ANGELA: Oscar! Oscar! Oh my God!
MERCEDES (*To RICARDO*): Cut! Cut!

(*RICARDO does and runs to OSCAR. MERCEDES stands still, frozen to the spot.*)

ANGELA (*Holding OSCAR's head*): What's the matter? Say something! (*She lets him down gently, runs to her bag, and takes out a bottle of pills.*)
RICARDO (*Trying to bring OSCAR around*): Old timer! Old timer! (*He takes his pulse and, alarmed, looks at MERCEDES. He goes down to her.*)
MERCEDES: What's the matter? What's the matter?
RICARDO (*Shaking his head*): He's got no pulse. I think he's. . . dead meat, babe. I'm going to call an ambulance. (*He starts picking up the lights and camera.*)
MERCEDES (*Starting to cry*): No. This can't be happening.
ANGELA (*While putting a pill in her husband's mouth*): Come on, come on, come on. . .
MERCEDES (*Approaching ANGELA*): What can I do? What do I do?
ANGELA: Leave me alone. Don't come any closer. There's nothing you can do now.
MERCEDES (*Paralyzed*): My God! This can't be happening! My God! What do I do?
ANGELA: Just go away, please. Get out of here once and for all.

(*MERCEDES grabs her briefcase and runs hysterically into the street.*)

ANGELA (*Massaging OSCAR, trying to bring him around*): Come on, honey. Come on. What's the matter? What's the matter? (*She very carefully tries to straighten out his legs. OSCAR lets out a light moan. ANGELA doesn't hear it and continues working on him.*)
OSCAR (*Shouting*): What are you doing, Angie? What the hell are you doing?
ANGELA (*Lifting her head and smiling happily. She gets very close to his face*): Oscar! What a scare you gave me! How do you feel?
OSCAR (*Between groans*): Help me sit up. Oh, my back!

ANGELA: You had a spell. Didn't you? I put one of your pills in your mouth.
OSCAR (*Trying to sit up*): Help me, Angie.
ANGELA: Yes. Here now. (*She does so with difficulty. OSCAR remains seated.*) Did you do any damage? Does anything hurt? Tell me.
OSCAR (*Touching his legs, he looks down at the landing*): Where are they?
ANGELA (*Trying to pull up his pants leg*): Let's see. Probably bruised yourself. Anyway the pants aren't torn. Does it hurt? Let's see. Move your legs.
OSCAR: Hold still, Angie! Of course my legs hurt. This is all that I needed, a fall like this.
ANGELA: You fell down very slow. Time enough to grab a good hold. You fell like from God's hand.
OSCAR: Where are they?
ANGELA: Huh?
OSCAR: Where are the TV people?
ANGELA (*Smiling mischievously*): They've gone, Oscar. I think they thought you were dead. If you could've seen their faces! That lady won't be back here again even if it means losing her job for life.
OSCAR: It was the railing.
ANGELA: Huh?
OSCAR (*Raising his voice*): The fault. It was the railing's fault. I felt my spell, Angie, that spell that I get sometimes, my heart. You hear me? (*She nods.*) I tried to hold on tight to the railing. I did, and I felt my fingers begin to slip. I couldn't hold myself up by it. It was like it was waxed, like they smeared grease on it. It was a trick, Angie. Touch it. You'll see what I mean.
ANGELA: The other time you fell on the step above. You remember? Just five steps from the landing. The other time you almost crushed me, Oscar. Today I fell on top. Better, since I don't weigh much. Poor darling.
OSCAR (*Noticing her ear*): Your hearing aid, Angela? (*Raising his voice.*) Where's your hearing aid?
ANGELA: Oh, I lost it. I think when I fell. Anyway, it didn't help at all.
OSCAR: That's crazy! Look for it. It can't have gone far.
ANGELA: We've been pretty lucky, Oscar. At our age, a fall like this. Good thing I have rubber bones.
OSCAR (*Raising his voice*): Find your hearing aid, Angela. I want you to be able to hear me.
ANGELA (*Looking half-heartedly*): I don't see it.
OSCAR (*Talking loud*): Look in the corners of the steps. On the landing.
ANGELA: Ah, here it is. I'm sure it broke when it fell.
OSCAR: Put it in. (*ANGELA puts it in her pocketbook.*) Damn it, Angela! Put it in!
ANGELA: OK. Boy, what a temper. That's a healthy sign. (*She puts the hearing aid in her ear.*) So, there. What now?
OSCAR: Help me get up. We've got to get out of here. Right now. We're not safe here.
ANGELA: Don't worry, Oscar. The TV people won't be back. I took care of that.
OSCAR: Look. Touch it. Touch the railing. It's slippery. Someone put grease on it.
ANGELA (*Touching it*): Well, I don't feel anything.
OSCAR: Feel it good.
ANGELA: It's new. Just varnished. That's all.

OSCAR: Mark my words, Angie. This is the landlady's doing. Another trick.
ANGELA *(She looks at him with a kindness and understanding)*: You're frightened.
OSCAR: She tried to do me in. But she didn't succeed. I'm still strong; stronger than she thinks. Come on. Help me get up. Let's get out of here.
ANGELA: All right. *(She helps him.)* Hold onto the railing with your other—
OSCAR: Never! *(ANGELA looks at him, worried.)* Forget there's a railing there. Forget the whole thing. It's like it was all a bad dream. Right?
ANGELA *(Helping him get up:)* There you are. *(After a pause.)* Only four steps and we're out in the street.
OSCAR: What are you talking about, Angie? Have you gone crazy? We're going upstairs.
ANGELA: Why? Don't you feel well? Do you hurt somewhere?
OSCAR: My legs and my back. And besides, this isn't going to end just any old way. I'm calling the lawyer right now, and we'll get to work. This wasn't done according to the law. Let's go upstairs, Angie. They tried to trick us, but it backfired on them.
ANGELA: Only four steps to the street, Oscar. We've never been so close as today. Come on. Let's go down.
OSCAR: What are you saying? Go out there now? Go out there now, and I'd be giving up my rights. Didn't you see how that TV woman tried to blackmail me?
ANGELA: I did. But we ruined the story for her.
OSCAR: So, maybe you believed the landlady paid for this? You believed that?
ANGELA: No. She didn't pay for it. I know that. But she got brought down a few pegs. She signed that paper and humiliated herself. What else do you want, Oscar?
OSCAR: I want to win this battle. I need this victory.
ANGELA: You've won it already. Morally, which is the important thing. Don't you see that?
OSCAR: Let's go upstairs. Help me. I don't intend to touch this railing again.
ANGELA *(After a pause)*: No. I'm not going to help you go up to the apartment.
OSCAR *(Incredulous)*: What are you saying, Angie?
ANGELA: I'm not going to take you into that prison again. *(She takes one step down.)*
OSCAR: Come here. Let me lean on you. We're going upstairs.
ANGELA: There're only four steps, darling. Four steps and the door to the street. You promised to go with me to that boy's fruit stand. You have to do that.
OSCAR *(Really frightened)*: It was a moment of weakness. I felt defeated. That horrible woman. That camera.
ANGELA: They're not here now. Nobody's going to film us going out. We're alone. Alone, like always. We got the railing. We got the landlady to admit we're right. There's no going back on this. I want. . . I need, I need you outside there. . . beside me.
OSCAR: I can't do it.
ANGELA: Why?
OSCAR: I can't get my legs to move. They won't move.
ANGELA: Of course you can. You've got to try.
OSCAR: I don't understand. You've never failed me, Angie.

ANGELA: Well, I can't say the same for you, Oscar.
OSCAR (*Shaking*): I can't do it. My legs are dead. I can't.
ANGELA: I'm saying you can. I'm asking you to try. I'll be happy with that.
OSCAR: Why? Give me one reason.
ANGELA: I already have.
OSCAR: Another one.
ANGELA: You know them all. (*Tears start from OSCAR's eyes as he stands silent. ANGELA comes close to him and touches him gently.*) I know. I know what you're feeling. But remember, you began this thing. You called the TV station. You. . .
OSCAR: Because I didn't know. . . I didn't know. . .
ANGELA: Quiet. You called them because you've always been a man brave enough to try things.
OSCAR: Until my legs gave out on me.
ANGELA (*Shaking her head*): I'm asking you now, for whatever time we've got left us, be that man again. . . show them you've got balls.
OSCAR: Angie!
ANGELA: Yes. Balls. And walk down those four steps with me.
OSCAR: I can't, Angie. Look, even my hands are giving out on me.
ANGELA: Just as far as the door to the street. Just to there. We'll walk down, we'll open it, you'll look outside, see the sidewalk. And if you don't want to go out, we'll go back home.
OSCAR (*Gone pale*): You promise?
ANGELA: I promise.
OSCAR (*In a whisper*): Let's go.
ANGELA: Thank you. Like you were doing it before. (*Handing him the crutch.*) You were walking real well. Real well.
OSCAR (*He looks at the railing distrustfully. He pulls a handkerchief from his pocket and wipes it insistently. ANGELA watches him and smiles.*) There, that's better. Angie, stand beside me.
ANGELA (*Doing so*): Let's go.

(*OSCAR, with a trembling gesture, starts down the remaining steps.*)

ANGELA (*Counting the steps*): Three. . . two. . . one. And we made it.

(*They walk to the door. ANGELA opens it slowly. A faint shaft of late spring sunlight floods in on the figures of the two old people. There is a long pause. A tense silence. OSCAR looks at his wife. He takes off his tie and puts it in his jacket pocket as the lights go to black.*)

THE END

CRITICAL REACTION TO THE PLAYS

"*Una estrella* (*First Star*) shows us the evolution experienced by the protagonist in a single evening, how she changes her way of seeing herself and seeing life. This is the kind of intimate, personal theatre that we seldom find. Theatre that goes straight to the heart and the emotions."

Javier González Soler
La Opinión (Murcia, Spain), March 1998

"*First Star* is an invitation to an inner voyage through the ghostly ocean of memory of a solitary woman. The entrance of a male character, an old friend of her father's, puts into motion the psychodrama that will develop throughout the rest of the work."

Juan-Antonio Vizcaíno
La Razón (Madrid), February 1999

What the protagonist "discovers is a male world so filled with physical horrors and a crippling sense of failure and despair that her father's past miscreant behavior becomes, to her, explicable. Hence, in the act of forgiveness, she finds herself, completes herself. . . . This is an incredibly powerful piece, especially so since it achieves its huge impact in so short a time."

Robert P. Arthur
Port Folio Weekly (Norfolk, VA), April 1998

"In *El pasamanos* (*The Railing*), the elderly protagonists are coerced into performing under the direction of a television journalist, whose self-serving attempts to theatricalize their lives make a powerful statement about commercial exploitation in the postmodern world."

Peter Podol
Entre actos (University Park, PA), 1999

The Railing "is the encounter of two characters who live a story in which we can all recognize our fears and our anguish."

Camila Schumacher
La Nación (San José, Costa Rica), 1999

ABOUT THE TRANSLATOR

Rick Hite is Professor Emeritus of Theatre/Communications at Virginia Wesleyan College. He is a graduate of Dartmouth College (A.B., Spanish) and holds degrees from The Johns Hopkins University (M.A., Spanish) and Michigan State University (Ph.D., Theatre). He was a Fulbright Lecturer in Spain in 1974-75. He is an actor and director and has worked in university, community, and professional theatre, and in film and television.

Rick Hite's staged translations include Alejandro Casona's *Siren Cast Ashore*, produced in 1963 by the Oak Grove Theatre of Virginia; Fermín Cabal and Pedro Almodóvar's *Dark Habits*, produced in 1996 by IATI at the American Theatre of Actors in New York City; Fermín Cabal's *Passage*, produced in 1998 by the Generic Theatre of Norfolk, Virginia; and Paloma Pedrero's *First Star*, produced in 1998 at Virginia Wesleyan College.

Translations by Rick Hite that have previously been published in ESTRENO Plays are Alfonso Vallejo's *Train to Kiu* (1996) and Cabal's *Passage* (1998).

TRANSLATOR'S ACKNOWLEDGEMENTS

I wish to express my deep and sincere thanks to Phyllis Zatlin, editor of this series. She is the editor *por excelencia*, and a translator's translator, always careful, always understanding, and always there. I also thank Kerri Allen and Margrette Thomas for technical assistance and formatting. And I thank Theatre Wagon of Virginia and ShenanArts for readings and workshops of both plays and Virginia Wesleyan College and the Virginia Commission for the Arts for making possible the American premiere of *First Star* in 1998.

Rick Hite

WESTERN EUROPEAN STAGES
Marvin Carlson, editor.

An indispensable resource in keeping abreast of the latest theatre developments in Western Europe. Each issue contains a wealth of information about recent European festivals and productions, including reviews, interviews, and reports. Winter issues focus on the theatre in individual countries or on special themes.

Published three times per year.
$15 per annum/$20 foreign
WES@gc.cuny.edu

Send subscription information with check or money order payable to
Western European Stages to:
Martin E. Segal Theatre Center
The City University of New York, Graduate Center
365 Fifth Avenue New York, NY 10016
MESTC@gc.cuny.edu

ESTRENO: CONTEMPORARY SPANISH PLAYS SERIES

No. 1   Jaime Salom: **Bonfire at Dawn** (*Una hoguera al amanecer*)
Translated by Phyllis Zatlin. 1992.
ISBN: 0-9631212-0-0

No. 2   José López Rubio: ***In August We Play the Pyrenees*** (*Celos del aire*)
Translated by Marion Peter Holt. 1992.
ISBN: 0-9631212-1-9

No. 3   Ramón del Valle-Inclán: **Savage Acts: Four Plays** (*Ligazón, La rosa de papel, La cabeza del Bautista, Sacrilegio*)
Translated by Robert Lima. 1993.
ISBN: 0-9631212-2-7

No. 4   Antonio Gala: **The Bells of Orleans** (*Los buenos días perdidos*)
Translated by Edward Borsoi. 1993.
ISBN: 0-9631212-3-5

No. 5   Antonio Buero-Vallejo: ***The Music Window*** (*Música cercana*)
Translated by Marion Peter Holt. 1994.
ISBN: 0-9631212-4-3

No. 6   Paloma Pedrero: ***Parting Gestures* with *A Night in the Subway*** (*El color de agosto, La noche dividida, Resguardo personal, Solos esta noche*)
Translated by Phyllis Zatlin. Revised edition. 1999.
ISBN: 1-888463-06-6

No. 7   Ana Diosdado: ***Yours for the Asking*** (*Usted también podrá disfrutar de ella*)
Translated by Patricia W. O'Connor. 1995.
ISBN: 0-9631212-6-X

No. 8   Manuel Martínez Mediero: ***A Love Too Beautiful*** (*Juana del amor hermoso*)
Translated by Hazel Cazorla. 1995.
ISBN: 0-9631212-7-8

No. 9   Alfonso Vallejo: ***Train to Kiu*** (*El cero transparente*)
Translated by H. Rick Hite. 1996.
ISBN: 0-9631212-8-6

No. 10   Alfonso Sastre: **The Abandoned Doll. Young Billy Tell.** (*Historia de una muñeca abandonada. El único hijo de William Tell*)
Translated by Carys Evans-Corrales. 1996.
ISBN: 1-888463-00-7

No. 11   Lauro Olmo and Pilar Encisco: ***The Lion Calls a Meeting.***
The Lion Foiled. The Lion in Love. (*Asamblea general. Los   leones*)
Translated by Carys Evans-Corrales. 1997.
ISBN: 1-888463-01-5

No. 12   José Luis Alonso de Santos: ***Hostages in the Barrio.*** (*La estanquera de Vallecas*)
Translated by Phyllis Zatlin. 1997.
ISBN: 1-888463-02-3

No. 13   Fermín Cabal: ***Passage.*** (*Travesía*)
Translated by H. Rick Hite. 1998.
ISBN: 1-888463-03-1

No. 14   Antonio Buero-Vallejo: ***The Sleep of Reason*** (*El sueño de la razón*)
Translated by Marion Peter Holt. 1998.
ISBN: 1-888463-04-X

No. 15   Fernando Arrabal: ***The Body-Builder's Book of Love***   (*Breviario de amor de un halterófilo)*
Translated by Lorenzo Mans. 1999.
ISBN: 1-888463-05-8

No. 16   Luis Araújo: ***Vanzetti.*** *(Vanzetti)*
Translated by Mary Alice Lessing. 1999.
ISBN: 1-888463-08-2

No. 17   Josep M. Benet i Jornet: ***Legacy*** (*Testament*)
Translated by Janet DeCesaris. 2000.
ISBN: 1-888463-09-0

No. 18   Sebastián Junyent: ***Packing up the Past*** (*Hay que deshacer la casa*)
Translated by Ana Mengual. 2000.
ISBN: 1-888463-10-4

No. 19   Paloma Pedrero: ***First Star & The Railing*** *(Una estrella & El pasamanos*)
Translated by Rick Hite. 2001.
ISBN: 1-888463-11-2

ORDER FORM

List price, nos. 1-11: $6; revised ed. no. 6 and nos. 12-19, $8.
Shipping and handling for one or two volumes, $1.25 each.
Free postage on orders of three or more volumes.
Special price for complete set of 19 volumes, prepaid, $90.

Please indicate below quantities and titles of plays: TOTAL

_____ _____   _____
_____ _____   _____
_____ _____   _____
_____ _____   _____
_____ _____   _____

                    Shipping & handling   _____

                    AMOUNT ENCLOSED   _____

Name and address: _____

                    _____

                    _____

                    _____

Make checks payable to ESTRENO Plays and send to:

ESTRENO Plays
Dept. of Spanish & Portuguese, FAS
Rutgers, The State University of New Jersey
105 George St.
New Brunswick, NJ 08901-1414

For information on discounts available to bookstores, contact:
FAX: 1-732/ 932-9837   Phone: 1-732/932-9412x25
E-mail: ESTRPLAY@rci.rutgers.edu
Visit out webpage at
http://www.rci.rutgers.edu/~estrplay/webpage.html